THE PHILLIPS GUIDE TO

CHAIRS

Published 1989 by Merehurst Press
Ferry House,
51-57 Lacy Road, Putney,
London, SW15 1PR

© Text copyright Peter Johnson 1989
© Copyright Merehurst Press 1989
By arrangement with Dunestyle Publishing Ltd.

Co-published in the United States of America by
Riverside Book Company, Inc.;
250 West 57th Street;
New York, NY 10107

© **Pictures**   Phillips Fine Art Auctioneers
Edited by   Emma Sinclair Webb
Editorial Director   Megra Mitchell
Art Director   John Strange
Illustration by   Richard Carr
Typeset by   O'Reilly Clark (London)
Separations by   Chroma Graphics (Singapore)
Designed by   Strange Design Associates

Printed in Italy by New Interlitho spa

ISBN 1-85391-064-3

THE PHILLIPS GUIDE TO

CHAIRS

Peter Johnson

MEREHURST PRESS
LONDON

Contents

*An illustration showing a Victorian day-bed
from* A Manual of Domestic Economy
*by J. H. Walsh, published towards the end
of the nineteenth century.*

Author's Note

The great majority of illustrations in this book were supplied by Phillips, the London auction house with a network of salerooms or other branches throughout the United Kingdom, in New York and in continental Europe. Phillips, in fact, handles more furniture than any other auction house in the world; therefore its spacious salerooms and cavernous cataloguing halls in Mayfair where I received guidance, information and friendship over many years from furniture specialists such as Michael Cowley, Philip Duckworth and the late James Pettifer were a storehouse of knowledge for this quest through the history of chairs, from their origins to their present day market fortunes.

I am grateful, also, to have been able to use illustrations from the auction archives of Sotheby's and Christie's (both in London and in New York), Bonhams, Henry Spencer and Sons, and the former King and Chasemore. Thanks for illustrations are also due to the Victoria and Albert Museum. The collecting game is a dynamic, living phenomenon and its developments are chronicled in the contemporary magazines of specialized appeal. I have been privileged to draw inspiration and information from writers, many of them old friends, in the pages of (among others) *Collectors Guide*, *Antique Collector*, *Antique Collecting*, *Antiques Trade Gazette*, *House & Garden*; from the past, I owe debts to *Art & Antiques* and *Antiques & Art Monitor*.

Throughout this book, where prices are quoted they are specified as the achieved auction price in a given year.

Introduction

ABOVE *Regency splendour uncovered: these chairs, each with a cartouche depicting a painted scene of a country house, are from a set of six found in a Welsh cowshed. They sold for £26,400 in 1985 and their story is told here.*

A disused, decrepit cowshed on a former farm in west Wales would be the last place anyone would look for hidden treasure. The auction house valuer from the big city was curious, however. He had been told something about 'an old group of chairs, probably worth nothing', which had been consigned to their rustic storehouse some years previously. Indeed, the family who owned them had sought the advice of another, locally based, auctioneer and had been advised to dump the chairs. Brought out into the light, one by one until there were six, and cleaned of dust, cobwebs and other cowshed detritus, the chairs 'simply shouted for attention', said the valuer. They were packed off to Phillips in Cardiff where in June 1985 they sold for £26,400, much to the astonishment of the owners; even the auction house was no little surprised, as it would have been pleased if they had made £10,000.

The cowshed had given up a superb set of beechwood chairs – four single and two elbow – dating from the Regency period (see illustration). Beneath the dirt, the paint on the beech was probably not original, but they were in fine structural order and the cane seating was in good condition, as was the delicate latticework in the horizontal splats (the central feature in the backs). What made the chairs so special, however, was the incorporation of a cartouche in the backrail of each seat, painted with the scene of a country house. Two of the backs bore an inscription, naming two houses; on others, thick paint had blotted out the inscriptions. The chairs, it appeared, had been in the same family since they were commissioned for a hunting lodge in around 1800 – for stylistic purposes deemed to be in the Regency period. The family was left to enjoy its windfall; the buyer, a West Country dealer bidding against national and international competition, was bequeathed the interesting task of identifying and researching each of the six country houses in England and Wales; and the public at large who read about the find in the newspapers was stimulated to ponder generally on the roulette of selling family heirlooms...and, in particular, on the prices for sets of chairs.

Chairs of Regency period are among the most popular. In this case, however, there was a premium on the value of the group. Several factors contributed to that bonus. The artistic addition of the country house cartouches made the chairs unique. The provenance of the hunting lodge and one family ownership was a valuable contribution. Quality of craftsmanship and excellence of condition (the cowshed, which was fortunately dry, had provided a benign environment, at a steady temperature) obviously added to the chairs' attractions, as did the fact that they formed a medium sized set. Then there was the frisson of their having been 'found', of a treasure hidden away and coming fresh to the market – something which even the most hardened dealers cannot resist. Finally, it must be said, the chairs were exceedingly comfortable to sit on: antiques that were to be used and enjoyed.

Prices for Regency chairs are now approaching those for eighteenth-century furniture. Rarity brings high values, and in their turn high values create more scarcity as owners of good furnishing antiques tend to retain them, in anticipation of ever rising values. For these reasons, and at a time when general awareness of antiques is increasing rapidly, the time frontiers of collecting are for ever being advanced. Here, it must be acknowledged that few people actually 'collect' chairs. Every household needs them, of course, but they are not amassed in the way that paperweights or watercolours or embroidered samplers are. Nevertheless, the 'collecting' idiom is relevant when someone sets out to furnish even piecemeal a house in antique or near-antique style. There are rules to be learned and discoveries to be made. Thus, furniture buyers can be said to have 'discovered' the nineteenth century in the last two decades. Periods which were unacceptable in the antique 'trade' or to the discerning 'collector' of the interwar years are now recognized as valid and important fields of interest.

In Britain many furniture specialists wrote off a considerable part of the nineteenth century -- as though Queen Victoria's coming to the throne in 1837 and the consequent development of the machine age ruled out any hope of worthwhile furniture being made after that date. A commentator on the Victorian aesthetic climate wrote at the turn of the nineteenth to twentieth centuries of 'the most tasteless ineptitude in nearly every branch of art', and his comments reflect attitudes which have long robbed the nineteenth century of its fair dues. Now, of course, not only have many Victorian furniture styles, and in this context Victorian chairs, come into their own as desirable pieces, but the newfound popularity has spread to Edwardian furniture, most of which, at its best, is derivative of Regency or Sheraton tastes.

The Americans have always been ready to accept more modern frontiers of collecting than their European cousins; in America periods and styles tended to trail their relative movements in the Old World. However, this absence of transatlantic synchronization has produced some fascinating American furniture as the design style of one era overlapped with the climate of thought of a following age. No better example is to be found than in the Windsor chair, with its half-dozen American variations on an essentially English design. In its land of origin this has always been regarded as a 'country style' and has not, therefore, been the target of as much experimentation by master-joiners as it has been in America.

Chairs, as much as any other branch of furniture, have owed their developments through the centuries to many factors, not least to the various foreign influences. English furniture history was guided greatly by the stylistic movements which took place under the monarchs of France from the middle of the seventeenth century to the end of the eighteenth century – 150 glorious years of full-flowered talent expressed in the most sumptuous furniture the world has ever known.

For sheer magnitude of events in architectural and furnishing design we must look first to the reign of Louis XIV (1643-1715) in France. This was the age of baroque, masculine magnificence which took its cue from the unrivalled splendours of the court. It saw the building of Versailles, which took six years and at one time employed 36,000 men and 6,000 horses. Chairs, tables and cabinets were on the grand scale, employing the talents of specialists in gilding, artists in lacquer and sculptors of marble. Ormolu bronze or brass mounts worked into designs of figures, animals and plants, decorated sets of huge chairs which were designed to be seen in the ensemble of complete room settings. The rooms themselves were sumptuous creations, gaining additional richness from tapestries, carpets, silks from Italy and Lyons, and superb porcelain. In 1685 Louis revoked the Edict of Nantes under which Protestants had received a measure of protection in Catholic France. It was to prove artistically beneficial to both England and Holland. French Protestant furniture-makers, glassworkers and weavers fled to those sympathetic countries and set up in business, and their talents were eagerly welcomed by the increasingly prosperous upper classes.

After the masculine baroque of Louis XIV, there came, under Louis XV (1715-1774), the stylistic period known as rococo. A common motif, in addition to scrolls and shells, was rockwork, *rocaille* hence rococo. It was the age of the voluptuous boudoir rather than the grand salon, and in fact many of the large galleries at Versailles were chopped up into smaller rooms during the reign of Louis XV. Straight lines were taboo; chairs took curving lines, their designs following the whims of court arbiters of taste, such as Madame de Pompadour and Madame du Barry. Much of Thomas Chippendale's later work was influenced by the French rococo style; however, he made no attempt to follow some of its worst excesses, for eventually it overstepped the bounds, indulging in meaningless trivia in its search for ornament at any price.

Logically, French influence should have reigned supreme in American furniture of the late-eighteenth century, as all things British were to be eschewed. Despite the War of Independence, however, Thomas Chippendale succeeded where George III, his ministers and generals failed. His *Director* book of designs was the bond which tied the American furniture industry to London, and two editions of it were already available when Philadelphia craftsmen adopted the Chippendale style in around 1760, some 15 years before the war.

Louis XVI began his reign in 1774 and departed headless in 1793. During his time rococo contortions calmed down considerably, although the feminine influence was still strong. The boudoir look continued to dominate. Painted walls with a silk sheen finish, cupids and rose chains were the forerunners of wallpaper. Small and delicate chairs, often employing marquetry inlays of rosewood, laburnum, holly and tulipwood, were universally popular in the high society. In furniture on the grander scale, the name of Jean-Henri Riesener stood high. With the title of *ébéniste* (cabinetmaker) to Marie Antoinette, he created lavishly decorated pieces, some of the finest ever made, in a climate of rich patronage. After the French Revolution of 1789 came the Terror which saw the clearing out of noble homes. Much fine furniture was thrown to foreign dealers at a fraction of its true value. The homes of the wealthy in England reaped a harvest. In France, rococo was dead; classicism reigned. The ideas of Greece and Rome were embraced with revolutionary fervour in the First Empire, and Egyptian influence spread after Napoleon's Nile campaign of 1798. On chairs, as on other types of furniture, a menagerie of griffins, sphinxes, lions, rams and eagles welcomed in the new century.

The author recalls, in the late 1970s, discussing with a foremost authority the relative shortages of fine English and French furniture – especially good sets of chairs – on the London market. In the opinion of Frank Berendt, a prominent London dealer, specialists in fine English furniture consistently faced a tougher problem in obtaining the right goods than those dealing in French furniture. 'There was, simply, much less a good English furniture than French,' he said. The social, political and historical conditions of eighteenth century England supported this argument. England's furniture output – initially produced in lesser quantities than in France – was heavily accented on the domestic side; the country's cabinetmakers did not enjoy to anything like the same extent the full flowering of wealthy patronage enjoyed by the *ébénistes*.

Where Britain gained, however, was in the sheer, dedicated acquisitiveness of its moneyed classes. As Mr Berendt put it, 'Britain became the greatest repository of fine furniture and works of art the world has ever known and still is.' He firmly believed – to encroach upon a related and frequently argued topic – that talk of an 'art drain' from the United Kingdom was 'misguided, misconceived, chauvinistic nonsense'. In the field of French furniture, for instance, he pointed out that Britain had, in the Queen's collection, in the Wallace Collection, in the Victoria and Albert Museum and in countless other collections, most of the best French furniture ever produced; and certainly more than they had in France. 'Any serious collector of fine French furniture, living in France, would have to come to this country to study his speciality,' he said emphatically.

RIGHT *The top rail of this Regency elbow chair is its most striking feature – brass inlay on rosewood, using stylized flowers. Note the unusual arm supports. The chair was one of a set of six diners which the market priced at £5,000 in 1983.*

The Oxford English Dictionary defines the word chair as: 'A seat for one person; now usually the movable four-legged seat with a rest for the back', also 'A seat of authority, state, or dignity; a throne, bench, judgement seat, etc.' Here, there is an echo from history, for as soon as the chair developed, in medieval times, it was immediately associated with authority and status. He who sat in the chair was the 'chairman', and the subordinates over whom he presided sat together on benches before him, constituting the 'board'. The earliest chairs were far from being easily movable. They were in fact oak chests to which a high back had been attached for additional comfort. It was only towards the latter half of the fifteenth century that chairs with legs came into widespread use. What happened after that, is the subject of this book.

'Chairs as Art' was the theme of an essay by the architectural and design historian Reyner Banham, who died in 1988. On the occasion of an exhibition entitled 'The Modern Chair', held at the Institute of Contemporary Arts, London, in the August of that year, Paul Barker, a reviewer in the *Evening Standard*, recalled Professor Banham's essay. The trouble with designers, Banham pointed out, is that they do not realize that the mundane act of sitting is the very least of the things that can happen to chairs: 'They are used by cats, dogs and small children for sleeping in; by adults as shoe rests, for polishing or typing. If upholstered and sprung, they can be used for trampoline practice; if hard, as bongo drums. They are persistently employed as stepladders for fruit picking, hedge clipping, changing lamp bulbs and dusting cornices.'

A few months after reading this assessment, the author happened upon the following gem of saleroom reporting in the weekly *Antiques Trade Gazette*: 'A set of eight Hepplewhite design mahogany dining chairs defied the attention of the family dog to set the top price of the day at what was for these Cornish auctioneers [Lambrays of Wadebridge] a much smaller-than-usual sale. Comprising two carvers [elbow chairs] and six singles with serpentine seats over splayed legs and H-stretchers, the chairs were particularly attractive for their carving which featured wheat-ear motifs, not only to the pierced backs, but also to the arms of the carvers. Unfortunately, the legs of several of the chairs had been gnawed by the vendor's family hound, but this failed to deter a West Country dealer from buying them for £4,300.' Professor Banham, had he known, would surely have been delighted to add 'teeth-sharpener' to the list of a chair's varied functions.

Chapter One
The Age of Oak

ABOVE *Photocall for veterans: seventeenth-century oak elbow chairs of varying styles (including, right, a double-seater) seen in the setting of an English country house. Several of the front stretchers show the mark of wear-and-tear, a badge of true age in oak seating. In 1977 these chairs sold (left to right) for amounts of £360, £400, £1,400, £420 and £720; oak prices, generally, have more than quadrupled since then.*

Records reveal that when Margaret, daughter of Henry VII, travelled north to marry James IV of Scotland in 1503, she complained that the stool given to her at a pre-nuptial banquet was 'not to hyr Ease'. The king is reported to have then offered her his 'Chayre', clearly the only one in the great hall of the castle. This snippet from a herald's journal holds clues to the furnishing styles of the day. While the lord of the house might have the luxury of a chair to bring ease to his back, and possibly his arms, lesser people made do with simple joined stools, benches and forms.

Indeed, in the Middle Ages oak benches were the earliest type of seat furniture for all, from mighty to lowly. These benches, and the tables at which they were placed, were given stretchers – functional lengths of wood which connected the legs and worked in two ways: first, they gave stability to the piece of furniture; second, they provided a convenient foot rest for the user who was thus given some insulation from the coldness of earth or stone floors whose bleakness might be mitigated only by a scattering of rushes. The marks of scuffing from generations of feet are a necessary attribute of old oak seat and table furniture.

At about the time the Scottish James was displaying gallantry to his bride, seat furniture in Tudor England was already undergoing a revolution. The details of these changes should be examined with regard to the popularity of oak.

Oak – durable, dependable, sturdy – is the most English of woods. In the sixteenth century the land was well-stocked with forests and oak remained the principal wood for furniture throughout the Tudor and Stuart periods. It was not until the juncture of the seventeenth and eighteenth centuries that it was displaced to a significant extent by walnut. There is relatively more top quality furniture extant from the century prior to 1650 than from the century which followed, simply because 'soft' walnut is much more vulnerable to the ravages of time than oak. For example, an oak piece stands up more staunchly to the punitive effects of modern central heating than does the more fancy, veneered furniture. Furthermore, oak furniture continued to be produced by rural yet, nevertheless, highly skilled craftsmen long after the so-called age of oak faded towards the close of the seventeenth century. Indeed, several authorities accord 'the age of oak' open-ended definition.

There are more than three hundred varieties of oak, the English species being *Quercus robur*, the common oak, and *Quercus sessiliflora*, the fruited oak. The colour of oak varies from brown to white, though its popularity in the twentieth century has sometimes suffered with the general misconception that it is a 'dark' wood; indeed, the darkness has all too often resulted from the thoughtless vandalism of insensitive polishing in Victorian times. John Evelyn, the seventeenth-century diarist and silviculturist, observed that it 'will not easily glew to other wood, nor not very well to its own kind'. Thus, oak stands on its own integrity.

As oak trees were being felled in vast numbers, Henry VII passed a law enforcing the preservation of the woods and forests. His daughter, Elizabeth, encouraged the largescale planting of oak. Ironically, Elizabeth's forests reached maturity about a century later, when the age of walnut had arrived for the furniture makers, and oak was being relegated to carcase construction and drawer linings in the joinery shops of fashionable London and other big cities.

Nevertheless, in the 1500s, oak – supplemented by some walnut, elm and bog oak which was blackened wood from ancient trees preserved in peat bogs – dominated English furniture (and ship) construction. It was to this background, then, that change and sophistication affected three basic kinds of English seat furniture which were in existence at the beginning of the sixteenth century.

The first was a logical development of the lidded chest (itself a descendant of the earliest piece of cabinet furniture, the Bible box). It was given panelled sides and back which turned it into seating of the settle type, with the retention of the box-seat compartment for the storage of linen or salted bacon. Italy had witnessed a similar natural progression which transformed its typical, massive, carved chest, the *cassone*, into a *cassapanca*, with the addition of low arms and back. In the warm climate of Italy the seat was built with a low back and arms, while in England the settle assumed a .distinctively tall style designed to protect the sitter from the chill of draughty northern halls.

High-backed English seats were carved with a repertoire of motifs, including Tudor roses, scrolls, dolphins, zigzags, interlaced strapwork and linenfold, a design which mimicked the orderly drapes of folded textiles and was much used in the wall panelling of Tudor and Elizabethan rooms.

Oak settle furniture encounters chequered fortunes in the present-day markets. Obviously, anything from the sixteenth century, especially when lavishly carved with contemporary motifs, commands a high price. But, seating of the settle type continued to be made through successive centuries. It lies at the heart of country furniture production and offers no great challenge to a moderately skilled carpenter. Settles belong to the farmhouse kitchen or the country inn, but have built-in disadvantages if they are incorporated

RIGHT How much more decorative is this seventeenth-century oak inlaid chair, one of the original coloured drawings by Shirley Slocombe for Percy Macquoid's History of English Furniture, *1904-1908.*

into different settings. As one Sussex auctioneer remarked, after a successful oak sale in which half a dozen settles had provided the only downbeat exceptions: 'What do you do with a settle in a home?' Its high-backed form dictates that a settle be placed against a wall – the only place for the piece, to prevent it from becoming an awkward room-divider.

The second type of seating to make significant strides in the sixteenth-century was the X-frame chair. X-frames have a lengthy pedigree, having been employed by the ancient civilizations of Egypt. Their adoption in medieval England arose mainly from the land-owner's practice of travelling from house to house. The 'joyned chair' had existed in the fifteenth century as a canopied piece of great height which stood on a small platform in the hall and from which the master could survey his household ranged on benches. Some of these hefty chairs were designed to be dismantled and placed in leather packing cases when the owner 'progressed' to his other homes or to

BELOW *Another superb Slocombe drawing showing double chairs from the age of oak. Note the versatility of design in the back cresting of the two chairs: cartouches in one to contain the initials of, presumably, the owner, and a delicate loop arrangement in the other.*

the homes of friends and vassals. They were cumbersome, took a long time to dismantle and reassemble, and involved the attentions of a considerable labour force. The X-frame, similar in basic design to the modern camp stool, offered a lighter, more convenient alternative which, nevertheless, could still be the vehicle for decorative

BELOW *The date carved below the crest of this oak armchair is 1656, placing it within the Commonwealth period. The flattened arms and the uncompromising under-tier are indeed characteristic of the Cromwellian period, but the decoration on the back is vigorous and rich – a sunburst medallion supported by an angel and rampant figures.*

embellishment fitting the status of the owner. Thus the X-frame was given a new lease of life in the mid-sixteenth century, by which time it had developed into a luxurious piece of furniture. Those examples occasionally appearing in the saleroom today are usually constructed from oak and are intricately carved. Loose cushions rest on webbing support, attached at each side to the rails of the chair. In the better examples the quality of the tapestry covering the cushions or even part of the woodwork is a match for the fineness of the carving.

Inventories show that Henry VIII had numerous X-frames,

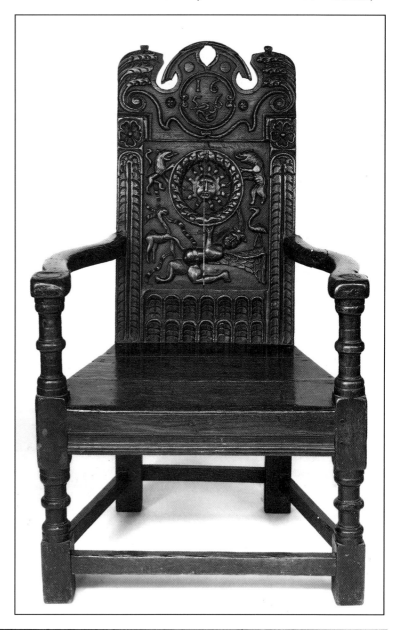

which were eminently suited to the voluminous fashions of the day and the King's ample girth. Elizabethan court notables vied with each other in commissioning expensive examples, consciously emulating the Queen's taste for opulent X-frame seating. Frames, as well as being carved, were often gilded or painted and revealed the influence of Italian fashions. Their popularity survived, and in Victorian days they were proudly displayed in the parlour as 'Hamlet seats'.

The third style to undergo design development during the sixteenth century was the 'turned' chair, which was to become the basic kind of seating in Elizabethan England. It was built of separate pieces, socketed together, and the turning was knobbed or ringed. In contrast with the panelled enclosure of the settle the chair was built with an open construction. The seat was usually of ample dimension to accomodate the fulsome fashions of the era. A raked back – sloping gently backwards – was adopted for additional comfort and the legs were united by stout, no-nonsense stretchers of thick oak; these were now raised 5 cm-8 cm (2-3 inches) above the ground, earlier ones having been positioned at floor level. Chairs built on these lines are commonly found with turned legs at the front and plain ones at the rear. Triangular seated chairs, to stand in the angles of walls, were also popular and were often constructed with sloping arms that swept down from the upper corners of the back.

Cushions were loose as upholstered chairs did not appear until late in Elizabeth's reign (1558-1603), and they did not become widely used until the seventeenth century. Large cushions of satin embroidery edged with gold and silver lace were popular furnishings for window seats (which also had a storage capacity) in Elizabethan mansions. An observer wrote in 1597 that 'the fashion of cushioned chayrs is taken up in every merchant's house'.

Refinements to the oak chair continued in the reigns of James I (1603-1625) and Charles I (1625-1649). The lathe was an important factor and the crafts of the chairmaker and cabinetmaker began to diverge as separate talents. Turning replaced carving as the principal form of decoration. The years of the Commonwealth (1649-1660) saw the emergence of a type of chair built on severe lines – with a leather back and seat. It is sometimes called Cromwellian, but it really owed its genesis to Dutch influences. Indeed, it is difficult to sustain the term 'Commonwealth style' for chairs – or any other type of furniture made in this period.

BELOW *Oak seating for the hall: an early eighteenth-century settle-type piece of furniture contains a panelled cupboard in the back for the storage of bacon or other goods. It also has trunk space beneath the hinged seat. Such 'extras' make it a very desirable piece of country furniture, with a value well into four figures.*

Chapter Two
The Market for Oak

ABOVE *Five oak aristocrats of the seventeenth century. All have simple, undecorated front stretchers at near-ground level, except the one second from the left, which sports a high-placed turned stretcher.*

The demand for good walnut and mahogany has never slackened. Indeed, the appearance of these woods on the market is tempered only by the scarcity of fine pieces. Sets of walnut and mahogany chairs find ready buyers and chase ever-rising price levels. Oak has had varying fortunes, and the market for artefacts made of this most English of woods calls for a special examination which will be the central subject of this chapter.

To understand the present state of the oak market one must retrace distant and more recent history. For about 200 years after the so-called age of walnut, oak was generally used for furniture in country areas. Great houses throughout the land remained basically furnished with oak, even if more fashionable walnut, mahogany and satinwood took pride of place in the more 'public' rooms. Rural production was important; indeed, many pieces of oak furniture on the market today come from the country workshops of Britain. This is good, sound furniture, reflecting the high quality of craftsmanship among regional joiners and carvers. Seat furniture is at the forefront of this supply.

In fashionable circles oak enjoyed a brief revival with the Victorian vogue for neo-gothicism, and again in the early years of this century during the flirtation with Tudor styles under the aegis of such arbiters of taste as Liberty. But, generally, oak had fallen into the doldrums until well into the third quarter of the present century. The

records of a Manchester auction house show that in around 1910 oak joint stools of the seventeenth century were selling for a few pounds each, and panelled chairs were faring little better.

Oak came back into favour towards the end of the 1960s. The growth of the country cottage habit helped, of course. Oak was the ideal material with which to fit out the 'second home' – country-style, utilitarian, and above all relatively cheap. There was a great deal of it available. After oak began to 'take off' the early 1970s witnessed a runaway boom in prices. Within the space of about three years some seventeenth-century chairs increased tenfold in value, at almost twice the average rate of all antique furniture. The basic reason was that buyers – trade and private alike – had woken to the fact that oak was underpriced compared with fashionable walnut and mahogany. Its durable qualities make it an ideal material to stand up to the buffeting of modern life and the stresses of central heating. Walnut, with its sensitive veneers, suffers badly in modern heating conditions – one reason for the popularity of oak among American home-furnishers. Since the oak boom of the 1970s, prices have levelled off, but the market remains steady, with healthy demand for antique chairs in particular.

Oak's new lease of life may have started off in the country cottages of Britain, but since then this type of furniture has moved back into town. Despite the fact that for some people oak carries

ABOVE *Seventeeth-century styles contrast sharply in these examples of oak elbow chairs. Considerably lighter in appearance and weight is the strikingly turned and triangular-seated version, with the theme of decorative uprights continuing to form an interesting feature below the seat rail. The carved chair displays a Garden of Eden scene in the back panel and makes lavish use of figures, grotesque beasts and scrolls.*

gothic overtones, it should be regarded as a light wood, with a rich and attractive patina; indeed, early English furniture fits in remarkably happily with present-day living styles. It blends surprisingly well with the lightness and coolness of modern 'Scandinavian' furnishing patterns, and is as well suited to a town house as to a farmhouse living room.

A magnificent country setting, however, is where oak looks its best. In the 1970s, Phillips, the auction firm, sold the contents of Horham Hall, Thaxted, Essex. The owners, a city mining director and his novelist wife, had moved into this 20-bedroomed pre-Reformation house nine years earlier and had then taken on the

BELOW *These oak elbow chairs sport the decorative designs handed down from the Regency period – elaborate scrolling and prominent lion symbols on the arms; they date, in fact, from the short reign of William IV (1830-1837). Solidity with style.*

daunting but rewarding task that would be appreciated by any lover of good furniture, given an adequate supply of money: namely, to fill the mansion with furnishings that would blend in harmony and style with a house that had been built by Sir John Cutte in 1502 during Henry VII's reign. In the magnificent Great Hall, dominated by its sixteenth-century window of armorial glass, Elizabeth I twice held court and once received the envoy of a prospective suitor, the Duke of Anjou. To furnish such a home was hardly a 'weekend cottage' project, but a long and expensive operation requiring careful planning. High on the list of furniture priorities was English oak.

The owners already had a nucleus of good chairs, mainly high-backed joined examples of the seventeenth and eighteenth centuries. The rest of the fine oak furniture they were to glean from Essex and Cambridgeshire antique shops and from careful search and buying in London and provinical salerooms. Here, we must briefly digress from chairs, because chairs – oak or any others – do not stand apart in furnishing schemes or histories but complement the cabinet, table and architectural furniture of the time and place.

The main bedroom acquired a rare Charles II oak and walnut chest. In the tapestry room were placed James II and William and Mary side tables and a beautiful pair of Charles II stools. A Charles II dresser and a refectory table dating from Cromwellian times were given pride of place among an array of oak in the dining room. Queen Elizabeth's bedroom required special treatment. The search was long and frustrating until a personal advertisement in *The Times* turned up a superb sixteenth-century oak four-poster – a bed fit for a monarch. Such a period treasure needs to be complemented by, say, a couple of seventeenth-century, low, nursing chairs, and – justifiably straying out of period on the grounds of comfort – an inviting Queen Anne upholstered armchair.

It is patently obvious that not everybody can furnish on this scale. But oak still holds out attractive buying oppportunities at a wide range of price levels. Nursing chairs, meant for mother or nurse, are attractively small, low-seated and have a gently sloping back which is often the vehicle for nice carving. Joined stools have a history and attractions of their own and are properly dealt with in Chapter Eight, on Stools.

Settle-type seating of oak is worth exploring. Apart from the big 'room-divider' type, which is difficult to accomodate in a domestic setting, there are smaller, less obtrusive versions which are highly desirable. Any settle-type seat which has an unusual feature is immediately enhanced in price. The shepherd's chair, for example: made extensively throughout the Midlands of England (and other country areas) in the eighteenth century, it has a high panelled back and drawer under the seat in which the shepherd traditionally kept lamb skins. There is also a piece which doubles as bacon cupboard and hall seat: it is something like a porter's seat with a high rectangular back enclosing a cupboard in which the bacon would be hung (decorative, fretted holes allow ventilation). If you admire fine old oak, are prepared to add a soft cushion and don't object to the smell of bacon, this proves a functional treasure and an investment.

BELOW *An example of eighteenth-century oak furniture with storage facilities. The seat conceals a chest in which linen would have been kept.*

Chapter Three
The Age of Walnut

Following the Restoration of the monarchy in 1660, with Charles II established on the throne (1660-1685), furniture took on a fresh aspect after the sobering climate of the English Commonwealth. Styles – of chairs in particular – were guided by the tastes of the court. In exile, Charles had surrounded himself with the nostalgic luxuries which he regarded as 'home comforts'. The renewal of acquaintance with his native land, however, came as a cultural shock to both king and subjects: he returned to a country where discomfort and suppression of decoration were associated with virtue. Court influences were to change all that.

In the royal furnishing schemes, Dutch, French and Italian furniture mingled with that of Portugal – the homeland of the Queen, Catherine of Braganza. The marriage had brought the dowry of Bombay, and eastern influences made themselves felt in English furniture in the form of carved ebony chairs inlaid with ivory. Skilfully tooled and cut leather work became a feature of English chairs, the style finding a perfect vehicle in the high-backed versions copied from

Portugal, which eventually assumed ornate patterned upholstery.

The high-standing chair, often with seat or back of leather or cane, was eagerly taken up by the English joiners, emulating the work of immigrant craftsmen who were patronized by the royal household and its circle of hangers-on. Gracefully proportioned panels of cane, set into the back, became a feature. Beech and walnut were now being used, representing a significant challenge to the traditional oak. Arms, on those chairs which possessed them, often ended in a downward scroll. Carving generally became more open – pierced carving replacing the solid form of the previous century. Later, under William and Mary (1689-1702), some of the more elaborate carving of Charles II's time was abandoned.

The stretcher connecting the front legs of a chair was raised or moved back, being no longer needed to support the sitter's feet as wooden floors and rugs had superseded cold stone and rushes. The joiner's inventiveness found a new, aesthetic role for the stretcher: elaborate carving made it a feature of ornamentation in its own right, now that it was raised or receded away from scuffing feet. But the stretcher, thus recently ennobled, was soon to vanish wholly from the fashionable scene – with the coming of the cabriole leg. First, however, two historical events were to have a dramatic effect on the development of furniture, proving once again that movements of the arts and crafts seldom, if ever, take place in a vacuum, uninfluenced by social or political happenings.

The Great Plague, which in London reached its peak in 1665, cast a sombre cloud over Europe. When the darkness lifted there was a reaction towards extravagance. This was reflected in the lifestyles of the more prosperous, and in their furniture. Extravagance was encouraged, of course, by the new climate emanating from court. An event then occurred which produced a watershed in furniture history. In 1666 the Great Fire of London brought devastation to the city and its people, destroying 13,000 homes and 89 churches. But, fearful disaster though it was, the fire was responsible for some beneficial effects. After the fire, English furniture experienced a rebirth; the reason was simple: London, the centre of the country's furniture inventiveness and production, housed much of the nation's fine furniture. With the destruction of so many buildings and the furniture they contained, the fire presented an irresistible challenge to produce new styles in a buoyant and extravagant mood that wanted to forget the Plague.

The second development which had far-reaching beneficial effects on art and design in England, came in 1685 and was prompted by political and religious considerations. It was in that year that the Catholic Louis XIV of France revoked the Edict of Nantes, which had given Protestants some protection against religious persecution. The decision and its aftermath drove thousands of Protestant French weavers, furniture and glass craftsmen to exile in Holland and England. Silk workers who settled in Spitalfields, London, built a silk and brocade-making industry which enriched the trend for upholstered chairs and sofas. This new heritage of talent asserted its influence during the reign of James II (1685-1688), but flourished

BELOW A late-seventeenth century high-backed dining chair is made in walnut, yet still resorts to an under-tier more in keeping with oak construction: baluster-turned legs and H-stretcher.

BELOW Again the stately, high-back look that was characteristic of many William and Mary walnut chairs. It sports an interesting, scrolled version of the cabriole leg and a stylish stretcher arrangement. The upholstery of seat and back is in crimson silk damask.

ABOVE *Seat furniture had taken a major step forward by the time of these early-eighteenth century walnut elbow chairs with the upholstered seat. The type of arm is known as the shepherd's crook. Cabriole legs end in claw-and-ball feet, derived from Chinese motifs.*

during the period of William and Mary, whose reign, not surprisingly, encouraged the adoption of Dutch styles.

With this background, England could not have been more receptively prepared for a new design that was to revolutionize the appearance and manufacturing technique of chairs – and even to change the wood material from which they were customarily made. For the establishment in general, use of the cabriole leg not only transformed the line of furniture (sofas, tables and even cabinets, as well as chairs) among fashionable circles in the provinces as well as in London, but drew the curtain on the age of oak.

The cabriole leg appeared from France in around 1680, although some authorities argue with justification that its route to England might plausibly have been via the Netherlands. Indisputably, the style really took hold in England when Dutch influences were being nourished under William and Mary. The outward-curved cabriole (or bandy) support is said to represent the leg of a leaping goat and its description comes from the Latin *caper* – goat. The style was first used on chairs and stools, and later on tables where it is equally effective. By the reign of the dual monarchs, the claw-and-ball foot, a Dutch importation, was readily accepted as a decorative appendage to the cabriole leg; the design, brought from the East by Dutch merchants, represents the Chinese symbol of a dragon's three-pronged claw clutching a sacred pearl.

(Although the year 1700 saw the claw-and-ball foot firmly established in England as an accepted fashion, American craftsmen of New England were not employing the style extensively until at least 40 years later. This is a classic example of American styles trailing those of Europe, often with interesting results. For the isolation of the American colonists from artistic movements in Europe was by no means always a disadvantage. Aspects of English or European fashion of, say, 30 or even 50 years earlier, could be used effectively in a new climate of furniture-making thought on the western side of the Atlantic.)

The coming of the cabriole leg made the stretcher aesthetically and structurally redundant – aesthetically for obvious reasons, structurally because the broad upper part and overall sturdiness of the leg provided ample support for the seat without the need for additional stability from cross-bracing. Above all, the new legs from Europe demanded a new material. The furniture-makers turned to walnut, a wood far softer than oak and easier to fashion in the required flowing curves.

Walnut, although widely used in Italy, Spain, France and south Germany during the Renaissance, was rarely used in England until the Restoration. Once regarded as a luxury wood for the wealthy, it was in much more general use by the end of the seventeenth century. It has strength without excessive weight, cuts and carves well and displays a rich patina. The 'glow' of old walnut, to be found on a Queen Anne chair, is the result of care and ageing. Furniture will take on a soft mellow tone and deep patina through exposure to the air, rubbing with wax polish and years of handling. It is to be deplored when this noble patina is removed by an 'improver' and replaced with brutal 'French polish'.

European walnut, *Juglans regia*, is a lustrous pale brown in colour, with brown and black veinings. Grown on the east coast of America, and eventually imported by Europeans as demand for the wood grew, was the species *Juglans nigra* – black walnut, displaying a darker brown colour, with even darker markings; it is much favoured by cabinetmakers fashioning pieces which present a large expanse of wood to admire.

England had walnut plantations of its own, but relied heavily on European imports. Here, southern England's 'hurricane' of October 1987 finds an echo in history: in 1709 a severe winter of lethal frosts and destructive storms in wide areas of Europe devastated many walnut trees. The English furniture trade's finest supplies came from the Grenoble area of France where slow-growing varieties produced wood marked by burrs, irregularities caused by knots or bough joints which made possible veneers with attractive configurations. Political insult was added to nature's injury when France banned the export of walnut. These setbacks encouraged the

ABOVE *The simple excellence of Queen Anne, mixing elegance with well-designed comfort, in a carved walnut-framed wing armchair. This type of furniture is ever popular and serves as well in a modern setting as it did in Queen Anne's day.*

ABOVE *From America in the mid-eighteenth century, a red walnut dining chair demonstrates the time-slip in design between the western and eastern sides of the Atlantic. Cabriole legs and vase-shaped splat are in full favour, but the maker is still relying on stretchers to unite the lower tier. Nevertheless this transatlantic cousin is a collectors' gem as eagerly sought in Europe as in its country of origin.*

ABOVE RIGHT *Curves proliferate in a George I walnut writing elbow chair: shepherd's crook arms complement a solid cartouche-shaped back and cabriole legs.*

transatlantic trade in darker walnut from Virginia, and may well have speeded the progression towards the fashionable use of mahogany. The eighteenth century's passionate love affair with mahogany, however, came later; and in the meantime walnut reigned supreme. Chairs made from the wood were to achieve their highest level of excellence and elegance during the reign of Queen Anne (1702-1714). Her day established such advances in a quintessentially English style – making the most of European influences and yet developing a national furniture identity – that her name is generally used to cover a period to about 1730, well into the Georgian era.

Queen Anne style was typified by cabriole legs. The feature became the vehicle for the carver's ornament, one of the few areas left to him in the new insular style. Some of the best carving of the period is to be found in elaborate and beautiful versions of the claw-and-ball foot and in acanthus leaf or other decoration on the knee. Elsewhere, there appeared to be little opportunity for the craftsman carver. Splats – the central, vertical part of an open back – were often straight or of vase or baluster shape. An American development was the banister-back chair, which retained the cane seat of its European ancestor, but incorporated four spindles in the high back. These spindles were usually rounded at the front, flat at the back. On both

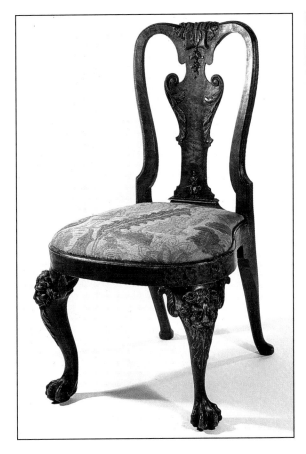

sides of the Atlantic there were slat-back chairs, with four or five horizontal slats, often painted a dull black.

The Queen Anne period produced an elegance of inornate quality and a dignity without severity. Alongside these attributes, more attention was being paid to comfort. Chairs generally became less tall and had rounded or hoop-shaped backs in happy proportions with the curves of seats and cabriole legs. Armchairs had their arms supported by an upright, placed a little way back from the front of the seat because the cabriole leg made it difficult to continue leg and arm support in one flowing movement.

In terms of comfort, a Queen Anne armchair, at its best, surpasses any product of any furniture-making period. Upholstered in fine silk or tapestry, it is the aristocrat of the drawing room. The chairmakers often provided wealthy clients with attractively-made cases, sometimes of leather, to protect the expensive upholstery. Thus, many a fine example has survived to the present day with its upholstery intact; lack of care would have meant rotted threads. Furthermore, our ancestors tended to prize their better pieces of furniture as a collector would; consequently fine armchairs escaped the wear and tear of general use. It is hardly surprising then, that Queen Anne walnut armchairs are highly-prized. Late in 1988 a

ABOVE *Elegance of proportion is seen in a George I carved walnut dining chair, with its vase-shaped splat of elongated form. An interesting feature is the shaped member connecting the rear feet, its function apparently being purely decorative.*

ABOVE LEFT *The solid vase-shaped splat in the back is an important feature of this George I carved walnut diner. Note the lion masks on the knees of the cabriole legs. Individually valuable, such chairs are worth considerably more pro rata when found in sets.*

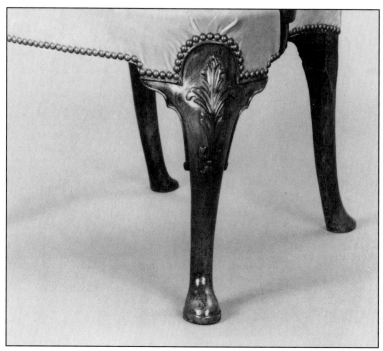

RIGHT *Detail of the leaf-carved cabriole leg and shaped pad foot of a Queen Anne walnut armchair, c. 1710.*

BELOW RIGHT *The essence of walnut; the essence of Queen Anne furniture: elegance of flowing line, married to serviceability. There is great harmony in the curves of the cabriole legs (on pad feet) and the line of the back, which is contoured to the human frame.*

BELOW *Cane is used to dramatic effect, allied with lavish walnut scrolling in this splendid chair of the William and Mary period. Note that the scrolling theme continues at the sides, giving a boxed-in, throne-like appearance to this substantial piece of furniture for drawing or dining room.*

LEFT *A pair of mid-eighteenth century
Portuguese rosewood chairs, remarkable for
the waisted cane panels in the backs. The
cane seats would have been covered by heavily
embroidered cushions. The cabriole legs have
particularly pronounced curves and are
decorated with leaf motifs.*

LEFT *One of the most comfortable chairs
produced in the history of furniture: a Queen
Anne carved walnut wing armchair. The
cabriole legs have scallop-shell-and-husk
decoration and end in moulded pad feet.*

bidder at a Christie's auction in New York paid $209,000 (£119,000) for one example, an extraordinary result which quadrupled the saleroom's estimate.

Marquetry – inlaid patterns of differently coloured woods – was as sparingly used on chairs as carving. Simple elegance was the order of the day, a quality seen in a remarkable country product of Queen Anne's time: namely the Windsor chair. Initially popular in the beech-woods of Buckinghamshire, it became fashionable elsewhere and has remained so up to the present day; its popularity shows no sign of waning. In Lancashire and Yorkshire, country makers were also developing their own chair styles, usually marked by distinctive arrangements of slats in the back. All these provincial enterprises are dealt with in Chapter Twelve, Country Seats.

In England, from about 1730, mahogany began seriously to challenge the supremacy of walnut. The wood-carver would soon be in business again. Chair-making was to take its place at the forefront of a new and even more glorious period of English furniture.

RIGHT *Comfort and style instituted in the Queen Anne period mark this George I walnut-frame wing armchair. Note the outswept scroll arm supports.*

LEFT *Eagles' heads form the terminals to the arms on these George II walnut chairs, a final touch of sumptuousness. The colourful upholstery is of* gros *and* petit point.

BELOW *These affluent-looking side chairs of Dutch origin from the mid-eighteenth century, are decorated in lacquered chinoiserie designs. Chinese influence, stemming from a thriving trade with the Orient, was reflected in much Dutch furniture.*

Chapter Four
The Age of Mahogany

ABOVE *A George II Irish carved mahogany elbow chair – provincial furniture, but from a practised hand. Notable features are the shepherd's crook arms and the wealth of carved embellishments, such as the shell designs of the seat rail and on the knees of the cabriole legs, which stand on claw-and-ball feet.*

ABOVE RIGHT *Part of a George II carved mahogany drawing-room suite in the French taste: solid bourgeois worth. The upholstery is in gros-point foliate needlework of a later date; it is rare to find household furniture surviving from the first half of the eighteenth century with its original upholstery intact.*

There could be some justification for the American claim, occasionally voiced, that mahogany was first used in the making of furniture in the Colonies. The claim is largely based on the evidence of New York and Philadelphia inventories which mention the wood at various times from 1690 to 1708 – before England's wholehearted entry into the age of mahogany, which is generally considered to have taken place in around 1720. Although mahogany was not imported into Britain from its native transatlantic home in any large quantity until about 1715 (the trade also received an enormous boost in 1733 by the modification of tariff laws), it is known that mahogany was occasionally made up into furniture in England in the latter half of the seventeenth century. Even earlier, Queen Elizabeth is said to have been mildly interested in the wood when some West Indian supplies were used by Sir Walter Raleigh to repair his ships.

The main genus of mahogany is *Swietenia*, first found in the West Indies and South and Central America. Later, another type, *Khaya*, came from Africa. The Spanish were quick to recognize the

qualities of the new wood which had great strength, variety of grain and figure, lent itself to high polish and was ideal for carving. There is even evidence of sixteenth-century Spanish Renaissance furniture being constructed in mahogany. In England the Cuban and San Domingo mahogany was preferred by joiners and cabinetmakers. It was good for carving and had an original light colour which gradually changed to a deep lustrous tone. Later, South and Central American varieties came on the market and, subsequently, in the nineteenth century, African mahogany was used; it was lighter in weight than the transatlantic varieties, softer, and tended to have some interesting striping effects.

The image of mahogany sometimes suffers, like oak's, from the epithet, 'a dark wood'. In America particularly, there were long-held opinions that it was essentially a blackish-red wood; this, in fact, was the result of dark stain and over-varnishing. Various trends in furniture design have left us mahogany in a variety of shades, simply because of contemporary fashions in surface treatment. Thus, good

ABOVE *A somewhat staid example of the designs of William Kent: the carved mahogany elbow chair has a comfortably serpentine-curved back. At the limits of its cabriole legs it has severely restrained block feet, which would not be to everybody's taste.*

ABOVE LEFT *This George III elbow chair has later been painted white with gilding touches; nevertheless, these do not detract from an attractive piece of seat furniture. The splayed arm supports are particularly appealing.*

ABOVE *An excess of 'busyness' marks this, one of a pair of George III Irish mahogany elbow chairs. Eagles' heads and a shell motif surmount the balloon-shaped back and the splat is alive with curves and carved decoration. The ornithological theme is continued in the arms. For good measure, the cabriole legs have foliate ornament and end in claw-and-ball feet.*

ABOVE RIGHT *A George III carved mahogany dining chair has a slightly ballooned back, enhanced by a moulded, serpentine top-rail. Its legs are simple, square and chamfered.*

English Georgian should have a light red-brown tone from polishing with beeswax. Mahogany of the Empire period, in the early part of the nineteenth century, was rich red and highly polished.

A couple of decades were often sufficient to see great changes sweeping through furniture design. The period between 1725 and 1750, encompassing the greater part of George II's reign (1727-1760), is a good example of such rapid evolution. These years represent a milestone in the nomenclature of English furniture periods. Prior to that time we tend to borrow the names of monarchs to describe furniture periods – from Elizabethan to Queen Anne. Afterwards, the picture changes. Admittedly, terms such as early, mid or late-Georgian (or even specific reigns) are in use, but through the golden age of English furniture, which spanned the latter half of the eighteenth century and extended to the Regency period, great movements and styles are known to us through the names of artistic and talented commoners, rather than kings and queens. For many people, England's furniture glory is summed up in three names: Thomas Chippendale (1718-1779), George Hepplewhite (died 1786) and Thomas Sheraton (1751-1806).

Their working era was preceded by a short period, the second quarter of the eighteenth century, which had influential effects on the movements which followed. An outstandingly important factor was the establishment of mahogany as the principal wood for fine

furniture. Secondly, there came the inspiration of architects such as William Kent, who was probably the first of his profession to make a practice of designing the movable as well as the fixed furniture of his rooms, as part of unified schemes.

Kent (1686-1748) was heavily influenced by the styles of Italy's Andrea Palladio (1508-1580) and those of his own fellow countrymen, Inigo Jones, Christopher Wren and Colen Campbell. Lavishly ornamented, Kent's chairs were seats for the rich and mighty. Cabriole legs were embellished with animal details such as lion, eagle, owl and human masks, claw-and-ball feet and eagle's talons. He revelled in chair decoration that included foliate scrolls, lions' manes, rocks and shells, satyrs and other mythological beasts. To this repertoire of design, he would add the final touch of magnificence – elaborate gilding.

His influence spread throughout the fashionable furniture-making industry. After the plain elegance of the Queen Anne style, there prevailed a widespread trend for carving lion masks on chair legs and arms, with the manes often covering the arm supports. Hoof feet were popular. Fish scales were used to decorate legs which might end in dolphins' heads. The eagle motif terminated legs and arms and surmounted the back rail of chairs, often with simulated feathers swathing every carvable surface. Women's classically sculpted faces appeared on the knees of chairs – and even American Indians' heads,

ABOVE *Matching upholstery at first glance appears to 'pair' these two George III carved beechwood elbow chairs in the French taste. Then the constructional differences become more apparent. There is harmony, however, between the curves of the cabriole legs sported by one, and the straight lines of the other's tapering uprights.*

ABOVE *Chippendale's 'square' look is demonstrated in this mahogany, upholstered armchair. From the Dutch he borrowed the broad seat; the cabriole leg and claw-and-ball feet were also inherited from earlier styles – and the Chinese inspired the design on the rose brocade upholstery. The chair was part of an important set of 10 which sold for £4,700 in 1969; the price would be multiplied considerably in the saleroom today.*

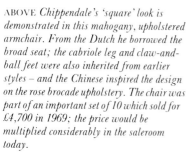

ABOVE RIGHT *From a drawing-room suite of George III giltwood furniture, comprising a sofa and a set of four elbow chairs. The upholstery has been replaced with a temporary substitute and the chairs have been regilded.*

whose feathered war bonnets provided challenging scope for the carver's talents.

The apron provided by the seat's front rail became the recipient of designs such as scrolling and shellwork. A popular motif was the acanthus leaf which has markedly serrated edges, a design found on Corinthian capitals and therefore in character with the classical flavour of the new Palladianism. Lavishly carved aprons were a hallmark of the work of Giles Grendey (1693-1780), a London master joiner who produced many pieces for export. While chairs were undergoing this decorative transition, they were growing wider in order to accommodate the large hooped skirts of high fashion. For the same reason, the arm supports were raked, or sloped outwards, to allow more open access to the chair's seat. Rich gilding would echo the golden panel surrounds of interior decoration; chair seat covers of Spitalfields velvet would match the lining of the walls.

In Kent's hands the medieval X-frame chair underwent some macabre transitions, which seems to support Horace Walpole's jibe that Kent's designs were sometimes 'immeasurably ponderous'. In the 1730s-40s the use of the X-frame was sometimes incongruous: for example, it might serve as the front legs of a busily-carved chair, while the rear legs were in the cabriole form – a combination far removed from the cool disciplines of Palladianism. Lack of harmony, however, does not prevent these X-frame chairs achieving high prices in the present-day salerooms. Other highly-priced relics of this period are lacquered, or japanned, chairs. The sap of a tree found in China, Japan and Malaya is the basis of lacquering. The sap is tapped like that of a rubber tree and, when dry, forms a semi-hard transparent film. The hard, dense surface achieved in oriental lacquering results from applying and then rubbing down many coats.

ABOVE *A Chippendale carved mahogany dining chair in the gothic style. The pierced, pointed-arch splats express the gothic theme, which is cleverly echoed by the square, chamfered front legs.*

ABOVE LEFT *Architect and designer Robert Adam created these chairs in a form known as* bergère. *They date from 1775-1780, reveal French influence, and sport temporary upholstery.*

It is a process that has little in common with modern lacquer, a compound of cellulose derivatives that are sprayed on by means of compressed air.

Kent's excesses apart, his success in satisfying a new market gives him a seminal role in eighteenth-century furniture design. Throughout the century there was a steady move away from the harshness of preceding centuries, towards a more elegant and refined way of life. Nobody made a greater contribution to this movement than Thomas Chippendale. It was the combination of mahogany and Chippendale's own designs that gave his furniture an everlasting appeal. Without mahogany the delicate, lacy quality of Chippendale carving would not have been possible.

Chippendale was the son of a joiner and picture-frame maker who had moved from the provinces to London. He relied solely on carving for decoration, rejecting all inlay work. His chairs were masterpieces of fine proportion and symmetry, varying from the more solid earlier creations on cabriole legs to his straight-legged versions, with intricate ribbon carving in the backs. Later still, he turned to the gothic style, with arches and tracery the main form of ornament in the backs. Chippendale students argue over the merits of each style and over which one represents the pinnacle of his design talents. For some enthusiasts, he reached the summit of excellence in chairs which interpreted the Chinese mood in geometric patterns.

His designs covered all forms of furnishings from bookcases to tea caddies. He shamelessly adapted the ideas of other people – the French, the Dutch, the neo-gothicists, the Chinese. Before his time, well-designed furniture was for the wealthy and privileged. Under his tutelage, good taste reached a much wider public. To a great extent, this more general availibility came as a result of his evangelism and

ABOVE. *Chippendale in the boudoir: one of a set of three George III carved and later-gilded occasional chairs,*

the printed word – Chippendale's own published work.

The first edition of Chippendale's design book, *The Gentleman and Cabinet-Maker's Director*, at £2 8s., was published in 1754 (the second and third editions in 1759 and 1762). It announced that his designs were 'calculated to improve and refine the present taste and suited to the fancy and circumstances of persons in all degrees of life'. His book was for the 'Gentleman and the Cabinet-Maker', to 'assist the one in the choice, and the other in the execution of the designs'. It was, in fact, a style book or catalogue, particularly valuable to furniture makers remote from day-to-day contact with London and its ever-changing fashions.

Examples of Chippendale's work are scarce because his work was avidly collected from an early date and tended to fall into the possession of the great families; extant pieces from the master's workshops are well documented. His followers produced many good copies, however, and their versions of the mahogany chair, with squarish back and straight or cabriole legs are the nearest that most people will ever get to real Chippendale. There are certain Chippendale characteristics which help a furniture expert to identify the handiwork of the master. Chippendale had access to a mahogany of excellent quality. With such good and ample material available, he never stinted on his carving; he carved deeply and he carved daringly. Thus his chair splats in the back are fashioned with a delicacy that often escaped the works of lesser makers. The proportion of space in relation to wood in a chair back was always well-balanced. Furthermore, Chippendale or those working under his direction would chamfer the wood of the splats from the rear to give them a more fragile appearance; this nicety might be overlooked by the maker in the country or abroad, working from a *Director* design shown in full face.

After the masculine baroque of Louis XIV (1643-1715), France celebrated the rococo style under Louis XV (1715-1774), and its fantasies of feminine elegance attracted the rich and the fashionable in England. Much of Chippendale's later work was influenced by the rococo, but he was sufficiently self-motivated to reject the worst of its excesses. Nevertheless, he borrowed for chair decoration some of the motifs of the French style such as rockwork (*rocaille* – hence rococo), shells and C-scrolls.

George Hepplewhite's origins are unknown. When he died in 1786 his widow carried on the business in London and two years later brought out his design book, *The Cabinet-Maker and Upholsterer's Guide*. His chairs are recognizable for their shield or heart shaped open backs, their elegant legs and their graceful curves. Unlike Chippendale, he did not eschew inlay. Settees had elaborately turned legs, and an extremely popular Hepplewhite motif was the triple Prince of Wales feathers.

The early designs of Thomas Sheraton, chronologically the third of the great trio, derived much from the styles of Louis XVI (1774-1793). In France the excesses of rococo had been tamed considerably, although the feminine influence was still strong. The boudoir look, light and delicate, continued as a principal theme. But the French Revolution of 1789 was followed by the Terror which saw the clearing out of noble homes; much fine furniture was disposed of to foreign dealers at a fraction of its true value. Rococo was dead; classicism reigned. Napoleon's Egyptian campaign of 1798 ushered in the new century and a plethora of sphinxes, griffins, lion motifs, claw feet and rams' heads were used as decorative motifs. All these were incorporated in chair designs. Sheraton, already influenced by the classical lines of the architect Robert Adam (1728-1792), one of four talented sons of a Scottish architect, now adopted the French design motifs.

FAR LEFT BELOW *Rich-red tan upholstery harmonizes with mahogany of deep lustrous patina in this example of a Chippendale dining chair crafted in the gothic style. A masterpiece of proportion, serviceable and highly coveted by the enthusiasts of Chippendale.*

LEFT *The gothic influence is seen in this dining chair produced in the Chippendale style. Interlaced scroll splats and a deep stuffover hide seat are typical of his designs. This chair comes from a set of 16 diners, of late Georgian vintage – probably early-nineteenth century. The chairs' fidelity to the master's style was sufficient for the set to sell for £35,000 in the mid-1980s.*

BELOW *From a set of eight, this Georgian mahogany diner is in the Hepplewhite style, showing to great effect his characteristic shield-back design. The splats have wheat-ear decoration, possibly indicating that the set was originally designed for a country owner.*

ABOVE *This Chippendale mahogany library chair uses as its central feature a lyre-shaped splat, which would make it just as well suited to the music room of a great house. The square, tapered legs end on unusual block feet, to which castors have been added.*

Sheraton's story presents an enigma: there is no evidence that he ever personally produced a piece of furniture to be sold (nor, for that matter, is anything known to exist which can be indisputably attributed to Hepplewhite's own hand). Born of a poor family at Stockton-on-Tees, County Durham, Sheraton moved to London where he and his family lived in perpetual hardship. Perhaps he tried to do too much. Besides being a prolific author of furniture and design manuals and an art teacher, he was a fervent and active Baptist preacher. Treatises on furniture in his *Cabinet-Maker and Upholsterer's Drawing Book* of 1791-1794 reflect his evangelical zeal. He frequently wrote outspoken criticisms of his furniture-designing predecessors. Of Chippendale's efforts, he observed: 'As for the designs themselves, they are wholly antiquated and laid aside, though possessed of great merit according to the time in which they were executed.' Of Hepplewhite's work, he wrote: '...if we compare some of the designs, particularly the chairs, with the newest taste, we shall find that this work has already caught the decline, and perhaps, in a little time, will suddenly die in the disorder...they serve to show the taste of former times'. He was not writing about some period of furniture fashion buried in the distant past, but within less than a decade after Hepplewhite's death. But, then, as we have seen, a decade can be a long time in furniture design.

A significant clue to the prevailing excellence of English furniture craftsmanship in the late eighteenth century lies in the printed material which sustained that industry – the design and drawing books, dictionaries and guides from the master arbiters of furniture style. In modern terms, the drawings would be considered totally inadequate as production patterns; many would be regarded today simply as sketches.

The reason for the sketchiness of detail, of course, is that by Hepplewhite's day the skills of the specialized joiners and cabinetmakers had reached such a level that these men knew intuitively what thickness was needed in a chair leg or a splat, how far a foot should be tapered, how deep the carving should be on a chair back. Drawings did not need to be explicit. If further evidence is required, one need only compare a surviving piece of furniture with the design book drawing on which it was probably based. The former is often infinitely superior to the latter in terms of balance, symmetry and proportion. When the vogue was for lightness, chairs would be depicted with shield backs of such airiness as to defy practicality. Pedestal desks, standing on corner feet only, beg for additional support. When Chippendale claimed that his skills could improve any design in his book by its execution into a piece of furniture, his boast was a true one, quite apart from being a form of salesmanship. Indeed, it is believed that some among Chippendale's prolific output of designs were never turned into furniture.

Sheraton was a master of scale, a talent which shows at its best in the beautiful chairs he designed and in the rectilinear cabinet furniture produced from his design books. Satinwood, of yellowish-brown colour, from trees in the West and East Indies, was his favourite wood. Occasionally he allowed it to be used with a carefully

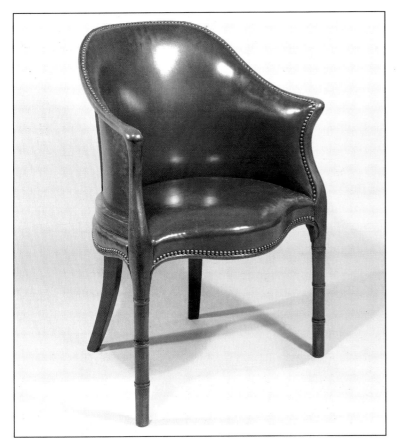

LEFT *A George III mahogany library bergère with arched back and serpentine seat rail. The legs are ring-turned. Brass-studded red leather helps give it an essentially masculine aspect.*

ABOVE *One of a set of six Louis XVI beechwood chairs, with ribbon-carved frames and upholstered oval-panelled backs matching their upholstered seats. The maker has chosen the simplicity of fluted, tapered legs. The set sold for £10,450 in mid-1987.*

LEFT *Dutch opulence: one of a set of six eighteenth-century marquetry dining chairs. Dutch marquetry, involving delicate inlays of variously coloured woods, was particularly florid and skilfully executed, normally appearing on heavy cabinet-furniture. With bird, vase, flower and scroll ornament, it is equally effective here in seat furniture.*

FAR LEFT *A stylish, straightforward chair-of-all-work, this Sheraton mahogany example has a deep stuffover seat and slender, reeded, tapering legs.*

measured amount of marquetry decoration in cabinets or on the backs of chairs. Tulip, apple and rosewood joined mahogany were his favoured repertoire of materials. Chairs had a fine, rectangular look, usually without stretchers in England, although stretchers are a distinctive feature of American furniture in the Sheraton tradition. Legs were finely tapered.

Identifying the sources of many late-eighteenth century pieces of furniture – chairs included – proves problematic. Descriptions abound with phrases such as 'Hepplewhite style', 'Sheraton taste', 'in the manner of', 'George III' or 'late-eighteenth century'. Such a blurring of definitions was the inevitable result of the propagation of designs through the various editions of the masters' source books. Sheraton, for all his poverty, had a mailing list which included several transatlantic cabinetmakers and at least one client in Russia. His influence lasted well into the nineteenth century.

BELOW *This George III carved mahogany dining chair is after a design by William Ince and Thomas Mayhew who produced* their *Universal System of Household Furniture* in 1762-63, in competition with *Chippendale's best-seller* Director. *The cartouche back is interlaced with gothic splats, and reeded fans decorate the cabriole legs. In the early 1980s a group of five such chairs realized £4,000, leaving saleroom-watchers with the opinion that the price might have been considerably higher had the chairs' proportions been more balanced.*

RIGHT *Jean Baptiste Séné, a French master furniture-maker flourishing in the latter half of the eighteenth century, was the creator of this Louis XVI giltwood* fauteuil *which expresses in superb craftsmanship the stylistic qualities of the period.*

FAR LEFT AND BELOW *An Adam period elbow chair, with later gilt decoration. It is in the Louis XVI taste. It owes much of its elegance to the reeded, tapering feet.*

LEFT *Another product of the American scene, this being a Federal inlaid mahogany side-chair originating from the school of Samuel McIntire, a Massachusetts furniture-maker who flourished around 1800. The delicately proportioned and inlaid shield back is immediately reminiscent of Hepplewhite's popular design.*

ABOVE *Transatlantic Chippendale: a mahogany wing armchair from New England, c. 1770.*

Chapter Five
The Regency

In the late-1970s sets of Regency chairs were trebling in price at roughly two-year intervals on the London saleroom market. They have since sustained a healthy rate of appreciation and are among the most popular chairs with buyers from both sides of the Atlantic. But, first, what is the period known in Britain as 'Regency'?

It has been described as 'the last major period in English furniture' by those pundits who argue that craftsmanship died with the opening of the Victorian era. But this definition is, at the least, an over-simplification. Regency was more a culmination of ideas, a fusing of various styles and a launching area for new schemes and trends based on the growth of the machine age. The term Regency is both insular and misleading. In England the period serves to take furniture to the 1830s and beyond. George, Prince of Wales, was regent for his mentally ill father, George III, from 1811 to 1820, before becoming King George IV. What we now know as the Regency period in furniture, however, extended much beyond those nine years. Developments, based on earlier foundations, were under way in the 1790s and the period as a whole extended to William IV's undistinguished reign (1830-1837) and indeed, arguably, encroached on Victoria's early years as monarch. As for the direct influence of 'Prinney' himself, this can be truly traced only to his sponsorship of Chinese styles, seen at their most sensational in the Indo-Chinese architecture and decorations of the Brighton Pavilion.

English Regency is the equivalent, chronologically and often stylistically, of the French Empire mode – that is, the First Empire of Napoleon I. Americans were developing their own styles and these, cross-influenced by movements in Europe, were responsible for some exciting schools of furniture, now referred to under 'labels' such as Federal and Late Federal.

The greater Regency period embraced the victories of Trafalgar and Waterloo. It was a time of heroism and patriotism, of the growing enrichment of the upper and upper middle classes, of lavish spending at one end of the social scale, contrasting with abject poverty at the other. Steam power and gas lighting were being widely introduced. Huge sums were spent on architectural improvements – although the period signalled the end of the great architectural designers – and equally astounding amounts were sunk in gambling and fast living. While Regency styles were expressed in the language of the rich they did, however, filter down to more modest households: the Windsor chair embodied important Regency characteristics of elegance, and country areas produced nicely proportioned, rush-bottomed chairs whose straight legs and minimum of decoration were in striking contrast to some of the worst excesses to be found in the houses of the very wealthy.

English furniture was usually veneered in mahogany, satinwood or rosewood, a richly marked favourite of nineteenth-century makers. Among other finely figured woods which enjoyed popularity was amboyna, a native of the Dutch East Indies and prized as a veneer for its configuration of knots and whirls. Zebra beech (painted black and gold) and kingwood all made their contribution. It was a time of brass inlay for ornament; marquetry was now out of fashion. Chairs reflected the prevailing influences of classical archaeological discoveries – mainly Grecian and Egyptian – alongside separate strains of style derived from chinoiserie and a gothic revival.

To understand how these styles developed in the first three decades of the nineteenth century requires a journey back in history to about 1775, by which time the neo-classical had superseded Chippendale's 'Director' style in all but country areas. The arch-priest of the neo-classical, receiving his inspiration from the excavations at Pompeii and Herculaneum, had been the architect Robert Adam. His influence showed in a varied vocabulary of ornament, most types of which found their way into chair design:

BELOW *The carved decoration on this Regency rosewood veteran is to be admired: a crest of acanthus carving surmounts the top rail, which is inlaid with profuse brass marquetry; scrollwork ornaments the seat rail and reeding follows the lines of the sabre legs. The buttoned, red leather seat is of the slip-in variety.*

LEFT *Chippendale gave the sitter plenty of room. His chairs were comfortable, engineered with thought for the human frame, as well as being commodious. This elbow chair has a slip-in seat and delicately carved scrolls in the back.*

RIGHT The Hepplewhite taste is again seen
in this carved mahogany diner from the
George III period. It has the shield-back
shape so typical of the master's work; in this
case it is in-filled with tracery, which helps
make the back the focal feature of the piece.
A set of eight fetched in excess of £10,000 in
1984.

ABOVE *One of a set of eight Regency
rosewood diners whose design seems to have
eluded attempts to control it. The curves of
back and arms seem to sit unhappily on the
sabre-legged under-tier.*

festoons of husks, honeysuckle motifs, urns, medallions and rams'
heads. By the time of Hepplewhite's period of influence, this
classicism was to be found in his favourite heart and shield-shaped
backs and the use of Prince of Wales feathers and wheat-ears in the
decoration. In 1783 the Prince of Wales appointed Henry Holland to
redesign parts of his residence, Carlton House in London. Much
French furniture was supplied, but a sumptuously decorated Chinese
room displayed a range of furnishing in the oriental style that was to
foreshadow the Regency period's love of chinoiserie.

Sheraton had a strong formulative influence on succeeding
styles of the Regency. Tapering legs and square backs accentuated
the vertical lines of his chairs, in contrast to Hepplewhite's heart-
shaped curves. The sabre leg was also a popular form used by
Sheraton and taken up by Regency designers. Sheraton's *Cabinet
Dictionary* of 1803 and his (unfinished) *Encyclopaedia* of 1804-1806 were

LEFT *This George III mahogany elbow chair in the French Hepplewhite taste – a felicitous combination – has an upholstered cartouche panel in the back. French influence has given the cabriole legs a particularly sinuous line, and they are topped with fan motifs.*

ABOVE *Double-functioning Regency design. a metamorphic mahogany library chair on sabre legs. A quick and easy adjustment turns it into a set of steps to reach those books on the higher shelves.*

already preparing the ground for styles of the next decade, by which time 'Regency' was in full flower. Chairs assumed arms bearing dolphin, eagle or lion heads, derived from antiquity. Otherwise carving was used sparingly. Chair frames, especially those of beech, were often stained black or painted. Lacquering was in fairly common use. In later years, prompted by a rapidly deteriorating popular taste for things Grecian, Sheraton introduced features which were characteristic of some of the worst excesses commonly associated with Regency furniture at its most grotesque. One chair described in a Sheraton design is 'composed of a griffin's head, neck and wing, united by a transverse tie of wood, over which is laid a drapery thrown easily over and tacked behind. The front consists of a dog's head and leg, with shaggy mane, joined by a reeded rail'. Another chair has 'two camels' or dromedarys' (sic) heads, with a drapery thrown over their backs, the legs of which form the back and feet of

ABOVE *Single chair (elbow companion illustrated opposite page, top right). Regency mahogany relies for decoration on brass stringing in the top rails, turning and tapering of the legs, and rope-twisted splats; the last being a legacy of Britain's sea-faring euphoria over Trafalgar and other naval victories which signalled the start of the nineteenth century.*

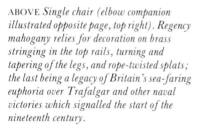

ABOVE RIGHT *A fine Hepplewhite carved mahogany* bergère *library chair of ample proportions. Note the refinement of leather-covered pads on the arms and the way the chair's considerable width has been exploited to make a prominent decorative feature of the serpentine front rail.*

the chair; the front is two lions with drapery over them also'. Imagine the craftsman-hours needed to produce these two chairs; imagine the furniture menagerie that would result from the craftsman's labours.

Hope there was, however – both in spirit and in name. In 1807 the architect Thomas Hope published his *Designs for Household Furniture and Decoration*, based on classical archaeological discoveries. Gracefully curved scimitar legs and curved back rails were favoured, although Hope's clients were also presented with a minor revival of the X-frame chair with its medieval echoes. During the following years, George Smith, in his *Collection of Designs for Household Furniture and Decoration*, struck a further blow for sanity by producing sensible, workable styles for ordinary homes, based on classical taste. Included were some designs in the Chinese and neo-gothic manner.

From the East, a new wood was making its challenge: bamboo. Much credit for bamboo's vogue is accorded to Sir William Chambers, the architect of Somerset House and designer of the famous and wildly successful pagoda in Kew Gardens. From the East, to which he had personally travelled, he brought the notion of using bamboo in furniture and he proceeded to publish designs to this effect. His ideas, especially for chairs, found some acceptance in the 1760s-70s, but it was the patronage of the Prince that really led to the realization of Chambers' visions of bamboo furnishing. Having been entranced for some years by Holland's Chinese room created at Carlton House, the Prince opened the door to a flood of Chinese decoration in the Brighton Pavilion. Popular taste, which hung on

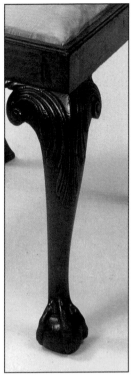

ABOVE LEFT AND CENTRE *A style much copied in the history of chairs: one of a set of six George III carved mahogany and fruitwood dining chairs in the Chippendale style. In contrast to the exotic choice of claw-and-ball style for the front feet, the rear feet are plainly finished.*

LEFT *A Hepplewhite period carved mahogany elbow chair, with a stuffover oval back and bowed seat. The splayed arm supports are finely decorated and the chair has reeded, tapered legs.*

ABOVE *Chairs do not exist in isolation, and here we see Regency ebonized and gilt-decorated elbow seats harmonizing with artefacts of other periods and other styles. The chairs are 'high' Regency, with cane seats and panels in the backs painted with scenes of reclining goddesses. The ring-turned, tapered legs complement the spindles in the back. In 1986 a set of four of these chairs sold for £7,150. The side table is early-eighteenth century, the mirror Chippendale, and the eighteenth-century Chinese mirror paintings have Chippendale-period carved giltwood frames.*

'Prinney's' every whim, embraced bamboo wholeheartedly. The fourth Earl of Poulett is on record as having ordered more than 100 pieces of bamboo furniture from a specialist maker. The rich furnished their 'Chinese' rooms with suites of seat furniture consisting of up to a dozen pieces. High-backed chairs showed off a harmonious mix of cane and bamboo, and the latter afforded interesting chairback combinations of splats and cross-rails.

Bamboo was expensive, but a cheaper alternative was at hand. Indeed, Sheraton, ahead of his time, had described in one of his design books how beech could be made to simulate bamboo. The joiners turned the beech so that it produced the distinctive knuckles of the oriental wood, then painters added the correct colouring and shading. Beech-bamboo had certain advantages over real bamboo, being firmer and allowing the furniture-makers safely to use traditional joining techniques, where the more conventional methods

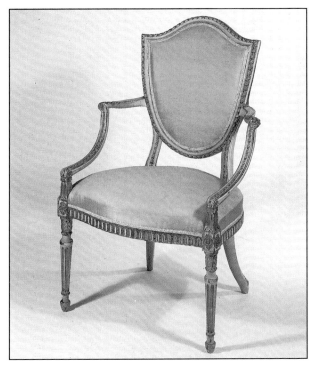

LEFT *Hepplewhite's shield-back supreme. Cream painted and highlighted with gilt, this elbow chair reflects the tastes of Louis XVI's court but is essentially Hepplewhite and English in form. A pair sold for more than £10,000 in 1985. Expect seats of such excellence to have made significant advances in value since that time.*

BELOW *A pair of Sheraton mahogany elbow chairs have reeded backs with trellis splats and curved bar top-rails. The ring-turned and reeded, tapered legs are typical of the style – much copied by chairmakers of the Edwardian period in the early years of the twentieth century.*

RIGHT *These beechwood chairs have been japanned – a process emulating oriental lacquering – in an attempt to turn the product of a country workshop into something fit to grace a grand house.*

BELOW *Requiring a grand setting that few homes can provide, these Regency carved giltwood armchairs are upholstered in crimson silk with gold flowerheads: stately seats for a formal environment.*

had a tendency to split and spoil bamboo.

Some of the most tasteful features of decoration on chairs developed out of the industrial, political and international events of the age. Industrialization in metalwork led to a trend for delicate brass stringing on rails and legs. Marquetry and carving declined in a period of Napoleonic wars which had increased the price of labour and materials. The lathe, for turning wood, had come into its own and was in universal use. Straight legs could be given added decoration by the inexpensive means of the lathe; if curved legs were to be decorated, this called for carving which was a much more expensive process. At sea, British naval power reigned supreme. Classic victories such as Nelson's at the Nile and Trafalgar led – despite the cost in carving – to a fashion for chair decorations in the marine tradition. Comfortable, functional yet elegant, chairs with rope mouldings on top rails and uprights, and soft leather seats, are often called Trafalgar chairs and are among the more desirable furnishings of the period. Anchors, cables, cannon balls, telescopes and dolphins were all to be found decorating chairs.

In the patriotic climate of a nation at war, such trends were understandable. More difficult to comprehend was the popular

BELOW LEFT *Mahogany with inlay of rosewood and brass produce a harmonious effect in this Regency diner with curved bar top-rails. A touch of rope-twist decoration in the uprights was typical of the post-Trafalgar era. The seat is upholstered in Victorian needlework; this part of the chair is most likely to suffer from the ravages of time. In 1987 a set of 10 such chairs sold for £10,000.*

BELOW *From a set of eight Regency ebonized and parcel gilt (partially gilded) dining chairs. The backs have Italianate landscapes painted on the top rails. The cane seats are typical. Copies – minus the delicately painted scenes – proliferated in Edwardian days, when the furniture maker looked back with nostalgia to the Regency era.*

RIGHT *Target of many an Edwardian copyist nearly a century later was this elegant, cane-seated elbow chair. In its Regency version here, it is cream-painted, with fine black lining.*

ABOVE *Brass inlay is used effectively in combination with rosewood in this Regency elbow chair, sporting a cane seat typical of much of the period's seat furniture. There is masterly use of arm curves in relation to the lines of the sabre legs.*

acceptance of French influences. Despite the general British hatred of Napoleon Bonaparte, it was his campaign in Egypt from 1798 to 1801 which gave impetus to Egyptian trends in the first decade of the new century (a staunch British patriot would no doubt have handed the palm to Nelson for his Nile victory). Sphinxes' heads appeared on chair arms, and, of course, Sheraton did not remain immune to the Egyptian fashion, as his employment of the dromedary heads reveals.

Adam's neo-classical vogue had suppressed eighteenth-century yearnings to return to the gothic, but the Regency period was to see a fresh turn towards the old style. This time, however, it was not to be the full gothic of the Middle Ages, but largely neo-gothic elements grafted on to modern styles. Other experiments produced dual purpose furniture, such as library steps which could be used as either table or chair. An era of wars brought forth sound, excellently-made campaign furniture, which relied heavily on the use of cane for chair

seats, light woods such as bamboo and beech, and metal hinges to allow pieces to be folded for the march. Many rare and exotic woods were exploited (Britain's seagoing fortunes kept open the lifelines of import), but there was, overwhelmingly, a popular preference for rosewood in English Regency chairs. Several species of tropical woods from India and Brazil are grouped as rosewood, so called from the odour of the newly cut wood. It is dense, heavy, resinous and of a deep red-brown colour, richly streaked and lending itself well to a high polish.

The 'conversation' chair was an interesting if somewhat freakish style dating from this era. A person sat on the shaped seat, facing towards what appeared to be the chair's rear, with his arms resting on the top rail of the back. It was, of course, a chair which could be used only by a man, but, given the long and expensive coat tails then in fashion, it had a certain practical use in preserving

ABOVE *Regency style in ebonized finish and gilt highlighting. The panels in the splats were vehicles for colourfully painted floral designs, now sadly faded.*

the uncreased sartorial elegance of anyone who sat on it.

In America, the aftermath of the birth of the republic saw changing centres of gravity in the furniture industry. New York, Baltimore and Salem, Massachusetts, grew stronger at the expense of Philadelphia, Boston and Newport. The most prolific and best-known name in American furniture-making is, of course, that of Duncan Phyfe (1768-1854). Born near Inverness in Scotland, he went to Albany, New York, with his parents when he was in his early teens. Later, with several years' experience of furniture-making .in the Hepplewhite tradition, he moved to Partition Street, New York, and there became a passionate follower of Sheraton. Soon the Astor family were his clients, his fame grew and he worked until the ripe age of 79, thereafter living in retirement. He is mainly remembered for the use of classical Greek styles, incorporating the lyre design for supports and chair splats, and animal legs and feet.

BELOW One of a set of eight George III carved mahogany diners in the Hepplewhite style, which sold for £4,400 in 1988. The rectangular backs and vertical splats – flower-decorated and formed as though to foreshadow the Art Nouveau movement – give the chair a distinguished look.

RIGHT AND FAR RIGHT *From a set of Regency mahogany and ivory-inlaid diners. These examples, part of a set of 10 (including a pair of elbow chairs), follow the style of Thomas Hope (1769-1831), author of* Household Furniture and Interior Decoration *which formulated archeological classicism for furniture. Greek key patterns decorate the top-rails; restrained use of brass mouldings on the seats complements the classical lines of the sabre legs. In 1988 the set sold for £26,400.*

LEFT *These mahogany dining chairs from the Regency period are gently understated in design. There is a minimum of brass lining on the back rails, and the simply-turned legs are in harmony with the chairs' rectilinear form.*

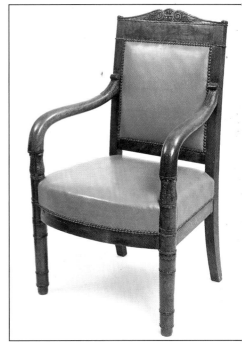

ABOVE *The maturity of the Regency period in England coincided with the French Empire style. This carved mahogany* fauteuil *is a typical example of the French fashion – classical lines with carving to give decorative appeal.*

Chapter Six
Victorian Values

In 1905 a popular writer on furniture took a wistful retrospective look at the nineteenth century: 'A great and growing school had followed the precepts of Chippendale and Hepplewhite and Sheraton. This glorious period of little more than half a century might have developed into a new Renaissance in furniture. Unfortunately, the early days of the nineteenth century and the dreary early-Victorian period, before and after the Great Exhibition of 1851, display the most tasteless ineptitude in nearly every branch of art.' Arthur Hayden (in *Chats on Old Furniture*) then went on to observe gloomily: 'It is impossible to feel any interest in the Windsor chair, the saddlebag couch, or the red mahogany chiffonier!' If we set aside part of this last statement as a mental aberration (how could anyone underestimate the Windsor, which was not Victorian in origin, anyway), we are left with a commonly expressed view of the time: that nothing good in furniture came out of the Victorian period.

Of course the late-eighteenth century and its immediate aftermath were together a glorious period of English furniture; of course the work of Chippendale, Hepplewhite and Sheraton remains a shining beacon. But to dismiss as tasteless ineptitude all that followed in the nineteenth century, is to adopt an elitist view which completely ignores the part played by man and machine in serving the needs of a fast-growing public with buying power, in a market no longer confined to the wealthy and privileged.

Victorian furniture is of a style that has comparatively recently been revived and, therefore, still qualifies in many respects as an 'undiscovered area'. Back in the serendipitous early 1970s, when metropolitan salerooms turned up their noses at sets of dining chairs they will now distinguish with a whole-page catalogue illustration, when even country auctioneers said they made bonfires of button-back chairs and sofas, there were pickings for the pioneering spirit brave enough to say all was not bad from the nineteenth century. After the great furniture age of the eighteenth century, standards inevitably fell in the machine-dominated Victorian age. The bad news was a lessening of restraint and discipline in design, the growth of mechanical carving and turning, and the huge demand that meant a relative decrease in the number of craftsmen available. Shoddy workmanship existed, to be sure – but the good news is that much of the shoddy, by its very nature, has vanished with time. Today the best of Victorian furniture – seat furniture in particular – is worth seeking, and against it much modern furniture is no match in terms of price, investment potential, serviceability and aesthetics.

Age of borrowed ideas: this is the epithet thrown at the nineteenth century; but if the ideas were good in the first place, the borrowing is justified. Hepplewhite borrowed from Chippendale, who was no mean plagiarist himself when it suited him. Sheraton developed the ideas of Hepplewhite. The style we know as Victorian cheerfully raided the tastes and teachings of earlier ages.

The Victorians adored papier mâché, *seen here in a chair, a small screen and other items. The chair is, indeed, a masterpiece of delicacy, showing the versatility of this 'plastic' material, much used in the nineteenth century for a wide-ranging number of artefacts about the home. The highly decorative coal scuttle is an example of 'japanned' metalware popular in the period.*

RIGHT *The great Victorian balloon-back: if any chair expresses an era's furnishing style it is this example of the nineteenth century. Its balloon-shaped back and well filled stuffover seat afford a high degree of comfort, ideal for Victorians who spent many hours sitting around the dining or parlour table. This example is archetypal, with its cleanly formed back and characteristically turned front feet. Prices vary widely according to quality and size of sets.*

The home of a wealthy Victorian businessman, towards the end of the nineteenth century, might contain in various rooms a whole retrospective catalogue of the century's furniture styles. Drawing room and bedrooms would have the feminine neo-rococo look that lasted for 70 years from the 1830s. The so-called neo-Elizabethan, more correctly neo-Jacobean, would fill the dining room and hall with heavily carved pieces. The library leaned towards the neo-gothic, given a lease of life by Augustus Pugin's furniture designs for George IV at Windsor, their religious overtones making a strong appeal to the middle classes. Neo-medievalism had its day, influenced by and influencing William Morris. Japanese and Moorish styles became popular. Art Nouveau enthusiasts struck away from revivalism and historicism. Heap the whole mass of Victorian styles together and the result can be horrific, unless it is done with panache and humour in the right setting. But from this eclectic collection of the century there are satisfying rewards for the person of relatively modest means wishing to furnish a home with the pickings of Victoriana.

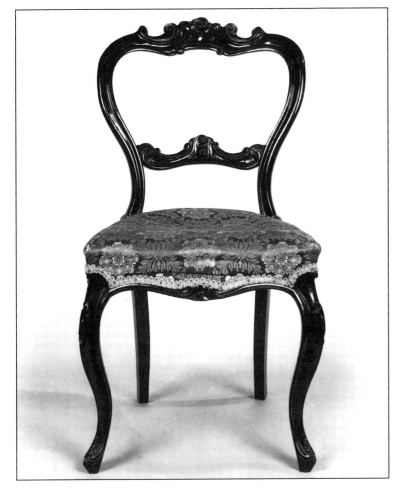

LEFT *A Victorian balloon-back. Carving and pierced work in the back rails, plus the use of cabriole legs complement the decorative upholstery. Sets of eight or more of such chairs are highly sought-after in present-day salerooms.*

Victorian balloon-backed dining and drawing room chairs in rosewood or walnut are highly popular. The balloon-back is among the most comfortable of diners. Its upholstered seat and the back's shape and gentle rake (backward slope) help make it so. It has elegance too: its waist is attractively nipped in, just above the seat and the plain back legs. Carving often embellishes the back and the front cabriole legs when the chair is meant for the drawing room, but these areas are left plain in most diner versions. In 1988, a set of 12 (a rare number) rosewood balloon-backs sold in a north of England auction for £5,000. Similarly, a pair of elbow armchairs, 'grandfathers' or the smaller 'grandmothers' will cost considerably more than double the price of a single example. The buyer can expect to apply similar mathematics to button-backs (which are no longer kindling material) when they come in pairs or other multiples, or as chair and sofa combinations.

Arms are absent from many Victorian easy-chairs simply because the woman's skirt was becoming extremely voluminous. Seated on a low chair whose upholstery was thickly padded and buttoned down at the back, she could relax in comfort and display to advantage her fine dress. Similarly, space was the essence in the design of the Victorian settee, a two-seater conversation piece, this, and not to be confused with the sofa meant for one person. A wooden-framed back, deeply buttoned and representing human embracing arms, was a feature of some of these settees sought by the ladies of high fashion.

It was the era of great exhibitions in crystal palaces – London, Paris, New York, Philadelphia and many other leading cities – and thus a distinctive type of 'public room' furniture developed, with fashion dictating its adoption in the home as well. There was the conversation settee, which sometimes appeared as a double armchair. Others would take the form of three seats with their backs to a central upholstered pillar. One version was arranged in a sort of conjunction which placed three people in the closest proximity and allowed them the maximum of intimacy. Popular in Napoleon III's reign in France, the design spread to Britain, where it appeared, richly upholstered, usually in Louis style or neo-classical; it was referred to as the *indiscret*.

The Victorians used large amounts of pine, as their forefathers had done. Characteristically a soft wood, it was largely employed for the carcases of cabinet furniture and as a vehicle for carving, notably in decorative country chests throughout Europe. Chairs, with the exception of inexpensive country versions, are not generally found in pine – which the English trade has insisted on calling 'deal', arguably in an effort to give the common wood a cachet that the true name lacks. There was a nineteenth-century fashion in New England for leaving pine furniture (including some ladder-back chairs of simple design) in its raw condition, or treating it to an oil finish which produced a dark tone. On the whole, however, buyers of pine furniture, from the seventeenth to the nineteenth century, required it to be painted, often in greens and blues, or stained to represent other woods. In the present century the desire to return to antique origins ·has resulted in a vogue for stripped pine, which reveals the wood's configurations, knots and all. Before the original process of painting took place, the furniture was bleached with a solution of lime; the removal of the painted layer at a later date exposes this whitened surface as an interesting-looking patina that speaks of age.

RIGHT *An early Victorian* papier mâché *armchair, for casual use around the home. To Victorians* papier mâché *was a passion; they believed they had invented it (which they hadn't) and gave it many uses, from prefabricated houses, through furniture, to coasters on the table. Such a chair, even an example like this minus its seating is today valuable, if it is in good condition.*

Chapter Seven
Victorian Vignettes

Designed more to impress than to provide comfortable seating is this Indian silver-gilt 'throne chair', dating from the second half of the nineteenth century. Having brought it home in triumph from India, where did the owner place it? It belongs more in an exhibition setting than in a home.

The makers of the traditional Windsor chair (see Chapter Twelve, Country Seats) discovered that heat and steam could be enlisted to provide its harmonious curves. Bows and spur-stretchers and backrails were fashioned by steaming the wood into a pliable state, bending it and clamping it into position. Thus bentwood was born. In the nineteenth century, Michael Thonet, of Vienna, master of bentwood furniture, was to owe a warm vote of thanks to the Windsor chair men. The combined talents – Austrian technical inventiveness on the one part, and traditional English craftsmanship on the other –

opened a new chapter of furnishing in the Victorian era.

The furniture designer Thonet (1796-1871) grasped the enormous commercial possibilities of making new furniture shapes possible by heating moist beechwood, particularly in the growing technological revolution of the mid-nineteenth century. To his technical skills he added marketing genius and, by the 1850s, he had established a London distribution centre which was soon selling a large quantity of bentwood chairs, tables with bentwood under-tiers and other furnishings to a prospering middle-class public.

His new furniture was a triumph of industrial design. Light, strong and attractive, the chairs were popular in hotels, shops, clubs and restaurants as well as in homes. Chairs for domestic use had caned seats, and sometimes a caned circular panel in the back. For restaurants, Thonet developed the use of the 'new' material, plywood, usually pierced by a pattern of small holes. (Many years later, by the time of the First World War, plywood for seating was to be improved by new techniques, involving thicker layers with their grains all running in the same direction and impregnated with resin for strength). Above all, the furniture was inexpensive, and by the 1860s it was in universal use, giving many a Victorian dining room a graceful touch so often lacking in the heavy, over-decorated furniture which marked much of the age. Here is one successful and lasting answer to those who claim nothing new and nothing good came out of the Victorian period.

The first bentwood furniture (as distinct from Windsor chairs with bentwood components) appeared in around 1830, but by 1851 it was sufficiently established for a Thonet table to be shown at the Great Exhibition in London. The table was in rosewood and walnut with a bentwood under-tier, whose bends and scrolls anticipated the designs of the Art Nouveau style to come. Thonet also exhibited bentwood chairs with cane seats and backs, not far removed in style from present-day 'Scandinavian' lines. The orders flooded in. Thonet's name reigned supreme in the new industry, yet it never became a household word with the public despite the universal success of his designs, which were as popular in Europe as they were in Britain.

Arguably the greatest triumph of bentwood was seen in its application to the rocking chair. Hitherto, the rocker had been made in the traditional form beloved by generations of Americans: a spindle or slat-backed chair (or even a Windsor) placed on a rocker underpart. Designers and makers who paid too little attention to the principles of balance could produce some near-lethal versions. Bentwood did more than ensure balance; it allowed the function of the chair to be expressed in its design: the rockers were carried up into the arms and into the back in one continuous serpentine movement. The rake of the back, the length of the seat and the curved under-tier gave it both comfort and stability. Perhaps its only disadvantage – if one were to seek a flaw – was that it demanded more room in the overcrowded Victorian parlour than the traditional squat rocker

The arrival of the bentwood rocker, of which Thonet designed many examples, led to a fierce marketing battle. Line illustrations of the new style dotted the furnishing columns of the press. In London a Thonet rocking chair was advertised in *The Graphic* of March 31, 1883 (12 years after his death), by Oetzmann & Company of London. It was of the usual gracefully curved style, but was given added comfort by thickly padded and buttoned-down back and seat.

The manufacturers of the traditional, upright rocking chair, particularly makers of the Boston rocker, replied vigorously with advertisements which extolling the solid virtues of 'the chair which won the West'. Again in *The Graphic*, an advertisement of 1884 advocated the 'Commonsense rocker' of traditional design. Readers were urged to take it easy in a Boston rocker specially adapted for rest and comfort. It was, said the advertisement, a chair 'specially recommended by scores of Gentlemen... The Ladies are enthusiastic... Graceful, Easy, Fashionable and Inexpensive'. The prices ranged from 25 shillings to 35 shillings. It was partly this American chauvinism about the 'log-cabin' rocking chair which prevented Thonet rockers from achieving the success in the United States that they had enjoyed in Britain. However, many bentwood versions were imported from Europe.

Rockers apart, bentwood furniture generally made nowhere near as big an impact in America as it did in Europe. At the height of bentwood's popularity, between 1850 and 1870, America was witnessing a rococo revival. One of its arch-priests was John Henry Belter, a fashionable cabinetmaker of New York. He undoubtedly knew of the steam process developed by Thonet, and Belter himself patented a laminating process which he employed widely in his rococo furniture, especially for chairs and sofas. This involved laminating together layers of rosewood, resulting in a plywood of great strength and pliability, ideal for the shell-like curves demanded by the rococo revival. Similar processes were used by another American cabinetmaker, Charles Baudoine. Here was yet another instance of America's frontier-bred society looking back to the past glories of European furniture styles and employing new industrial techniques to bring those styles to a wider public. And if bentwood found no great place in American hearts, neither did that other fashionable material of the nineteenth century, namely *papier mâché* (of which, more later).

Nevertheless, in Europe designs which flowed from the inherently plastic idea of bentwood were translated into other new materials employed by nineteenth-century furniture makers. Metal, was a prime example. There was a natural progression to curvilinear chairs of iron and brass and, later, steel tubing. A curved brass-frame rocker was actually unveiled at the Great Exhitition, an oddity of furniture design at the time but the forerunner of shapes to come three-quarters of a century later. Indeed, as recently as the 1930s bentwood was the inspiration for the chairs of designers such as Aalto of Finland and those adventurous makers who found a ready sales market through Heal & Son and other go-ahead London stores such as Liberty's.

Heal's, famous for its beds from early in the nineteenth century, was eager to seize on the new, attractive and light bentwood furniture.

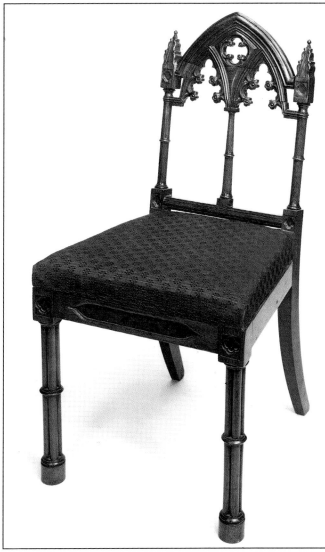

In the heyday of Victoria's empire, the military and colonial administrators were valued customers of the firm. No traveller's kit was complete without the addition of Heal's portable furniture for campaigning. In 1854 Heal's advertised campaign tables and chairs of bentwood with these words: 'The peculiar advantage of the above equipment is that it can all be packed on the back of a Horse or Mule.' To complete the campaigning package, a light bentwood saddle was also supplied.

Bentwood is bought and sold in the major salerooms of the present day, but it has not achieved the eminence of that other light and adaptable furniture material, bamboo. In the nineteenth century, however, it frequently 'stood in' for its more exotic and expensive counterpart as furnishing fashions resulted in the

ABOVE *A nineteenth-century library chair, boldly reflecting the neo-gothic taste in its double-arched back and distinctive front legs. This example comes from a group of seven sold at Phillips' dispersal of the contents of Stonor Park, Henley-on-Thames, Oxfordshire, in 1976.*

ABOVE LEFT *The Windsor chair found much employment around the Victorian home. This is a particularly attractive nineteenth-century example, with the much admired bow-shaped stretcher uniting its turned legs.*

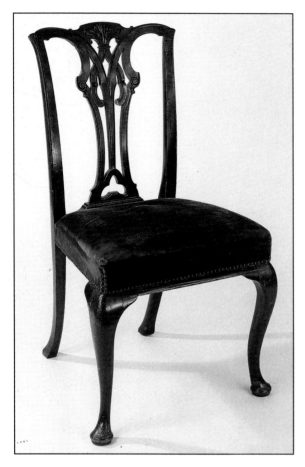

ABOVE *The Victorian era borrowed from countless earlier styles of furniture. Of the nineteenth century, and looking back nearly a century in time, is this example from a set of 12 dining chairs in the Georgian taste: sound serviceable workhorses of the dining room, much in demand for modern 'period' furnishing now that true eighteenth-century furniture has become comparatively inaccessible owing to its scarcity and price. Such sets have fetched several thousand pounds, depending on the quality of carving; this is still a fraction of the price of the genuine article.*

interesting simulation of a number of typically oriental styles.

If bentwood was the rage in mid and late-Victorian times, the fashionable hostess of the early-Victorian period could have boasted that the chairs on which she sat, the bed in which she slept, her sofas, piano, tables, firescreen and the exquisite trays on which food was served were all made of paper. Nobody could have sold the status-conscious Victorians the idea of mashed up paper as the source of elegance in the home, so they called it *papier mâché*, which sounded daringly foreign and *à la mode*. Fashionable it was, new it was not. *Papier mâché* came to Britain from France in the seventeenth century. There are records of picture frames made from it in as early as 1672, but the British vogue for it did not become a national craze until early in Victoria's reign when it seemed to provide a convenient answer to current furnishing fashion.

A newly-rich public wanted fluid lines, moulded forms and rich decoration for its money. *Papier mâché* could be moulded into shapes that would have cost dearly from craftsmen in wood. It could be mass-produced for a burgeoning market. Its high-gloss combination of painting, mother-of-pearl inlay and japanning – or varnishing in a way to imitate oriental lacquer – introduced a riot of colourful birds and flowers into thousands of gloomy parlours. It was light, delicate and graceful. *Papier mâché* faded from popularity, as fashions do, when a new fashion arrived on the scene. The advent of the crinoline in about 1870 called for heavier furniture styles; frivolous *papier mâché* fled before an avalanche of late-Victorian stodge.

The material was made from paper mashed up with glue, chalk and water, and sometimes fine sand. This pulp mass was then boiled down and, when it had cooled sufficiently, was moulded on oiled wooden shapes and baked in an oven until hard – so hard, in fact, that it could then be sawn like wood. Why turn to mashed paper when there was still plenty of wood about? The reason lies in the continental cabinetmakers' search for imitation oriental lacquer furniture. The Japanese and Chinese used to dry out their beautifully lacquered cabinets naturally in the warmth of the oriental climate. Dutch, and some French, furniture men in the seventeenth century had to resort to heated rooms and even ovens for the drying-out process. But the wood warped and cracked, spoiling the lacquered surfaces. A substitute had to be found which would stand gentle baking.

In England one of the greatest names in the *papier mâché* business was Henry Clay, who patented a process in Birmingham in 1722, some 70 years before the Victorian boom. Later, he did a roaring trade in trays in Covent Garden, London, and became 'Japanner in Ordinary to His Majesty'. Jennens and Bettridge (sometimes finely painted as 'J & B' on the edge of the decoration) is another distinguished Midlands firm whose work is much sought by today's collectors.

There was little that the Victorians did not make in *papier mâché*. Chairs tended to be of the open type, without arms, to accommodate the ample skirts of prevailing fashion. Around the home artefacts ranged from pill boxes to large wardrobes. Even houses were made in

LEFT *Victorians demanded value for their money. This mahogany dining chair – one of a set of eight that sold for over £5,000 in 1986 – emulates the richness of high-Georgian style: elaborately carved vase-shaped splats embodying a grotesque being's head, lion masks on the knees of the cabriole legs, paw feet, and dragons' heads on the arms – a menagerie of stylistic gimmicks to delight the heart of a nineteenth-century home-furnisher.*

LEFT *This settee with ecclesiastical presence was part of a suite of early Victorian gothic-revival furniture which also came out of Stonor Park, a house with much religious history. It is painted white and gilt, and is after a design attributed to Sir Charles Barry, c. 1845. The suite had an unusual list of component parts: eight settees, a pair of armchairs, a pair of stools and a bishop's armchair. In 1976 the whole sold for £1,150; but today the value would be far higher.*

RIGHT *One of a pair of carved mahogany and gilt-embellished open armchairs in the French taste. The upholstery is of early-nineteenth century French tapestry and its decoration represents mythical beasts. Substantial bourgeois comfort for the man of the Victorian house.*

the material: prefabricated sections were shipped out to the tropics where they were assembled by empire-builders. Probably the largest type of item to appear in the saleroom would be a four-poster bed.

It has taken more than a century for *papier mâché* to come back into its own. Even in the 1970s it hardly raised a ripple of interest in the salerooms, but today good pieces that have survived its banishment have an irresistible gloss for collectors. For all its sturdiness, *papier mâché* requires care. It should not be subjected to excessive heat, and damp warps the material. Nor does it like strong sunlight. Fakes are often of wood with a genuine but thin covering, or they are late-Victorian apologies for *papier mâché* made of cardboard sheets glued together and crudely japanned. The genuine article has a faint but distinctive smell, a slightly musty aroma, immediately recognizable by the expert. It also has a hollow sound when it is tapped, different from the more solid thud of knock on wood.

No account of nineteenth century furnishing vignettes would be complete without a reference to the *Biedermeier* style of Germany, dating from the first half of the century and based on the French Empire style. It was essentially designed for the lesser nobility and the bourgeoisie, imitating the magnificence of furniture to be found in

the grander houses of the rich and powerful.

The term *Biedermeier* was originally a derogatory nickname, composed of the common surname *Meier*, the equivalent of Smith or Brown, and the adjective *bieder*, which can be translated as meaning plain, worthy, modest, inoffensive, even stodgy. There was, in fact, a comic-paper character called *Papa Biedermeier*, the symbol of substantial German comfort and well being – *gemütlichkeit*. In *Biedermeier* furniture architectural themes and classic ornaments are given homely interpretations. Chairs and sofas have a comfortable pomposity; what once would have been eschewed as pretentious is now sought-after (at a high price) for being robust and bold. Carved details are curiously represented in black or gold paint. There is great play of padded backs and stuffed seats. Much mahogany is to be found, but *Biedermeier* enthusiasts also cherish suites in pear, other fruitwoods, walnut, maple, birch and beech. There is nothing stodgy about the present day fortunes of *Biedermeier*.

ABOVE *Simple country elegance, Victorian-style. The undeniable attraction of a set of chairs seen together is apparent in these early-nineteenth century spindle-back diners in elm. Their visual delights are enhanced by rush seating, unfortunately covered by cushions in this photograph.*

Chapter Eight

Stools

ABOVE *The decorated friezes seen on this pair are common to the set of five seventeenth-century joined oak stools to which they belong. The turned supports are nicely proportioned. The grain reveals a warmth of colour, belying the commonly held belief that oak is 'a dark, featureless wood'.*

In many people's minds the archetypal stool is represented by a rugged survivor of the seventeenth century, made in oak, with flat top, its four turned legs united by plain stretchers some 5cm-7cm (2-3 inches) from the ground. The apron, joining the stretchers at their tops, may or may not have some carved decoration. This type of joint, or joined, stool (in old inventories sometimes 'joynt' or 'joyned') was in popular use on both sides of the Atlantic, honest and solid, made for seating people at the long table. A key component of the jointing technique was the insertion of stout willow pegs for greater security. The stool's creation was the result of teamwork: the joiner would be responsible for making the frame of the stool and the carpenter would add any decoration that was needed – such as carved embellishment to the apron.

After 1650 the English stool was given an upward projection at the rear to form a rudimentary chair known as the back-stool, but the joint stool's lease of life continued long after this development. Marks of wear on the stretchers, as we know, are often a sign of age, having been made by the feet of countless sitters. A further test is to turn the stool upside down for signs of wear on the underside of the stretchers as these low stools, when not in use, were often stacked on the stretchers of the great table.

Such a joint stool is often called a 'coffin stool', a name derived from the practice of placing coffins on a pair of stools in church or during 'lying-in' at home (there are references to stools being used in churches as early as the twelfth century). In July 1661, Samuel Pepys mentioned in his diary his 'uncle's corpse in his coffin standing upon joint-stools in the chimney in the hall'. Indeed, the term 'coffin stool' is thrown around with abandon by some dealers, in reference to many a stool which never saw the inside of a church or supported the late-lamented. Sadly, in the case of church stools, years of placing porous flower-vases on them have ruined the tops of many; restoration is a job for an expert and can be expensive. Sadly, too, many churches have had to lock up their stocks of old joint stools to protect them from burglars who know only too well how valuable they are in the present-day market.

As a pair, the value appreciates disproportionately, but a word of warning is necessary here. Buyers should be wary of two such stools whose resemblance to each other is too close. The craftsmen of old never turned out two absolutely identical stools (or chairs, for that matter), and that applies as much to the work of the 'greats' – Chippendale and company – as to the humble country makers. Stools or chairs which match too closely in sets should start warning bells ringing: it could mean that they are in whole or part later reproductions, dating from times when machines had introduced a finer degree of exactitude into the business of furniture-making.

A further check against fakers is available: there is a proportion inherent in sixteenth and early seventeenth-century furniture which escapes the modern copyist. Testing a seventeenth-century stool for size will quickly demonstrate how the human frame has increased in stature over the centuries, and the discomfort of much early seat furniture will be apparent. It is known, for example, that the average citizen in Elizabethan England was of much smaller stature than his twentieth-century descendant. In modern times the planners of a replica Shakespearian Globe Theatre on the south bank of the River Thames had to revise their seating design fundamentally. They had wanted their tiers of benches to follow exactly the dimensions and spacing of the Bard's day. They discovered, however, that this was impossible as a twentieth century audience needed more leg room, the Elizabethan's thigh bone being on average 5cm (2in) shorter than that of his modern compatriot. This phenomenon is reflected in the scale of old joint-stools, which have a delicate, almost miniaturized, quality to them.

In the summer of 1988 a pair of oak stools, dating from around 1640, appeared at Sotheby's, Sussex, and more than doubled their estimate at £7,000. Measuring 58cm (1ft 11in) in height, they had attractive baluster supports, were of good colour, and had few tell-tale signs of restoration: a fine pair of joint stools at a regal price. Serendipity, however, still turns up the odd one in a neglected corner of a general antique shop. There are, happily, a fair number around

Basic seating in the seventeenth century: oak joined stools showing a rich patina of age. Stools such as these were sometimes used in churches for supporting a bier, and hence are often termed 'coffin stools'. Wear and tear showing on the stretchers can be a rough test of antiquity. These two sold for around £1,000 each at auction in 1987.

– a tribute to their strength and reliability of workmanship, which has stood the test of centuries.

Prior to the seventeenth century the stool was used universally. Chairs became the most common form of seating relatively late in the story of furniture. In the Middle Ages they were reserved for the heads of households or visiting dignitaries, the custom being for the high-ranking to be seated on chairs, while the rest of the assembly made do with benches, stools, or even rush mats on the ground. Among the earliest stools, always of oak, were three-legged examples, with the legs driven into round or triangular seats. In a will of 1463, a worthy living to the north of London referred to 'three fotyd stolys' kept in a spruce coffer.

The joint stool, however, became widely popular from the sixteenth century onwards, sometimes complemented by stools with X-shaped under-tiers, which had been familiar since ancient Egyptian times. In the homes of the wealthy, there were foot-stools of oak or walnut, made more comfortable with the addition of a cushion. Through the sixteenth and seventeenth centuries, in fact, cushions and, later, integral upholstery for seating were becoming more common. Indeed, co-ordinated furnishing patterns began to appear in the homes of the more fashionable. Stools appeared in walnut or gilded and painted beech, upholstered to match sets of chairs. Few examples remain, as it is thought likely that the stools were thrown away when the upholstery wore out. Durable, simple oak survived to be passed down from generation to generation. Furniture historians often have to look to old inventories and wills to delve into a lost world of carved and richly upholstered stool furniture. From the reigns of Charles I (1625-1649) and Charles II (1660-1685) there are records of many stools and footstools upholstered to match chairs and used in much larger quantities than the larger pieces of seat furniture.

ABOVE *These oak joined stools date from the periods of Elizabeth I (left) and James I.*

From the Restoration onwards, the form of stools – leg shapes, style of carving, upholstery – followed the fashions of chairs. When turned legs gave way to the cabriole, stools followed suit; walnut became the popular wood, to be partly superseded by mahogany. Whereas only the front stretchers of chairs were generally decorated, however, both front and back stretchers were richly carved on stools, which had to function 'in the round' of course. Noel Riley, writing in the magazine *Art & Antiques* in August, 1974, drew a graphic picture of entire new industries (import and cottage, professional and amateur) growing up on the desire for more elaborate stools, which were scattered round homes in profusion; the developments she traced reflected not only furnishing trends but changing social mores:

'By contrast to the plain and sturdy oak joint stools which furnished the homes of the less wealthy, these carved walnut or gilded beech stools with upholstered tops became more sumptuously decorated and more heavily stuffed with the approach of the eighteenth century. Velvets and silks, often brocaded with metal threads, were imported in large quantities and were used for furnishing and upholstering in the homes of the rich, while industrious ladies grew ever more enthusiastic in embroidering their own woollen chair and stool coverings in exuberant flower and figure compositions in tent stitch, or in the brilliant geometric patterns of

ABOVE *This pair of George III carved mahogany stools with scrolled, undulating seats, recalls memories of the X-frame under-tier – but with a difference. Indeed, the under-tier is a distinctive and rare feature of this pair. Similar stools are believed to have been supplied to an Oxford college by Thomas Chippendale in 1764. In 1986, the two were valued at more than £8,000.*

RIGHT *A Charles II carved oak stool, demonstrating the significant advances in comfort and refinement which had been made since the simple, oak joined stool was in universal use. The stretchers, in particular, and the legs have become vehicles for elaborate decoration by the carver, and the slip-in seat has tapestry upholstery.*

the fashionable and decorative Florentine embroidery.

'The eighteenth century brought still more comfort in the form of upholstery and needlework coverings for chairs, as well as in actual seating habits. The stool began to lose its place as a major item of seating furniture, as winged chairs, settees and day-beds began to appear in response to a new moral climate which allowed the rich to lounge comfortably about their houses. Stools are rarely mentioned specifically in eighteenth century trade-cards. They were evidently included in the expression "all manner of chairs and cabinet work" which many furniture craftsmen used on their cards.'

The changing role of stools became more apparent after about 1750. They were produced in smaller numbers, although they continued to be used in conjunction with sets of settees and chairs. Individual types were designed to complement the dressing table and the piano, or to be scattered in furnishing patterns along walls and in window alcoves. Until the mid-eighteenth century, walnut remained popular. In Queen Anne's time, for example (1702-1714, with a stylistic 'extension' which encompassed the first Georgian reign to 1727), the wood was often combined with gilded gesso, a plastic preparation used for raised decoration, to create a rich effect; other stools were japanned (in the manner of oriental lacquer) or of plain wood bearing bold carving on the legs and feet. Curves were now

ABOVE *A pair of Chippendale-period carved walnut stools with stuffover seats, on cabriole legs. The knees of the legs are decorated with acanthus leaf and C-scroll carving.*

ABOVE *Stools from the reigns of (*left to right) *Charles I, Charles II and James I. They exhibit the surprising wealth of carving and ornamental turning which may be achieved in such a basic type of seat furniture. Note particularly the deep carving and outline-cutting of the frieze and stretchers on the James I example, a stool of grace and fine proportions.*

favoured, with the sweeping line of the cabriole leg, scroll or claw-and-ball feet, and the use of shaped seat rails. And, of course, with the beginnings of the mahogany love affair from as early as 1730, this wood was appearing on stools, sometimes as a veneer on a beech or oak carcase. The cabriole leg became the vehicle for a wide vocabulary of decoration – masks, scrolls, shells, husks and ornate acanthus leaves.

Oddly enough, Chippendale did not include designs for stools in his *Director*, although there is evidence of their sales in his account books. While the use of dining stools declined steeply, the design book of Ince and Mayhew, the *Universal System* of 1759-63, offered 'lady's dressing stools' in the then popular rococo style. In his *Guide* of 1788, Hepplewhite recommended scroll-end window stools, 'peculiarly adapted for an elegant drawing-room of japanned furniture'. Large stools to seat two people were arranged informally against the walls of drawing-rooms or in corridors and galleries, often accompanied by foot-rests. By about 1800, John Best, a cabinet-maker, upholsterer and auctioneer of St Columb in Cornwall, was listing these larger items in his trade literature as 'conversation stools': the fashions of gossipy London society had spread to the remotest parts of the country.

Towards the close of the eighteenth century, the turn to neo-classical forms was interpreted in stool design through fluted, tapering legs and carvings associated with the movement. The demand for gothic styles and chinoiserie had its effect, and by Regency days stools were returning to the X-shapes of ancient Greece

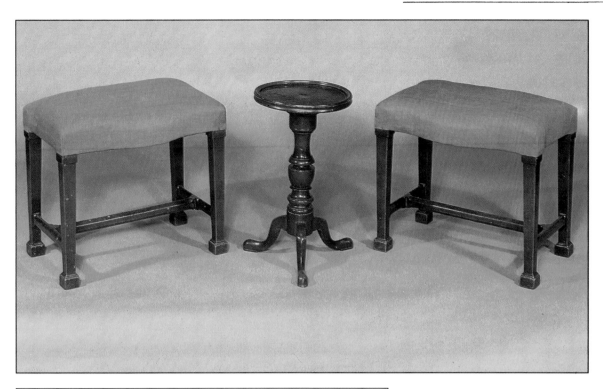

ABOVE *A simplistic form – not far removed from the outlines of the much earlier joined oak stools – marks this pair of George II mahogany stools with stuffover upholstery. This pair sold for £7,000 in 1984.*

LEFT *A typical oak joined stool in the style of the seventeenth-century. Those found in churches and used to support coffins have often had their tops discoloured and rotted by having porous flower vases placed upon them.*

RIGHT *Liberty's of London registered the design of this stool in 1884, a year after its Furnishing and Decoration Studio was established under Leonard F. Wyburd. Now a treasure of the Victoria and Albert Museum, London, it is known as 'The Thebes Stool' and is on a walnut base with a concave leather seat. Its Egyptian lines were extremely popular with the buying public who flocked to Arthur Lasenby Liberty's emporium of good taste and adventurous innovation in Regent Street. Versions of the stool came with matching cushion, and in mahogany and oak.*

and Egypt. Many became vehicles for the most elaborate carving: dolphins, lion masks, cupids, hounds and dragons. The utilitarian value of the stool was now being shunned; instead it was regarded as a vehicle to display its owner's wealth, status and taste: Smith's *Household Furniture* in 1808 advertised such exotic stools as being 'intended as ornamental extra seats in elegant Drawing Rooms'.

Victorians loved footstools. These small accessories – round, oval, square or rectangular – would be scattered around in quantities. They were often decorated in Berlin woolwork with pastoral scenes. Other types were covered in velvet or beadwork. Larger stools were scattered about in decorative profusion bordering on clutter. But practically the only stool a Victorian actually sat on was the piano stool: a wide, scroll-ended variety whose seat lifted to reveal storage space for sheet music; or else the late-Victorian circular-topped revolving stool which could be raised or lowered mechanically to suit the height of grandmama or little Polly.

Walnut and mahogany stools of the eighteenth century are highly prized and priced today, reflecting the quality of the construction and decoration. Rare examples, complete with their original upholstery, can run into many thousands of pounds. All too often, however, the original upholstery is entirely missing, has been extensively restored, or is in deplorable condition. Such defects, of course, reduce a stool's value considerably – and repairs and restoration by a skilled craftsman are extremely expensive. Regilding and repainting are also detrimental to a stool's value, as is the replacement of legs or feet. As in any other branch of antiques, the buyer of an old stool should sound out the best professional advice available – from trusted dealer or established auctioneer – before purchasing an example. Oak joint stools are, on the whole, much less expensive than some of the more elaborate pieces which came later in furniture history. But even these, when they are prime examples of the old stoolmaker's craft, and come as a pair of beautifully proportioned and unaltered specimens, can almost match the prices paid for the best oak furniture.

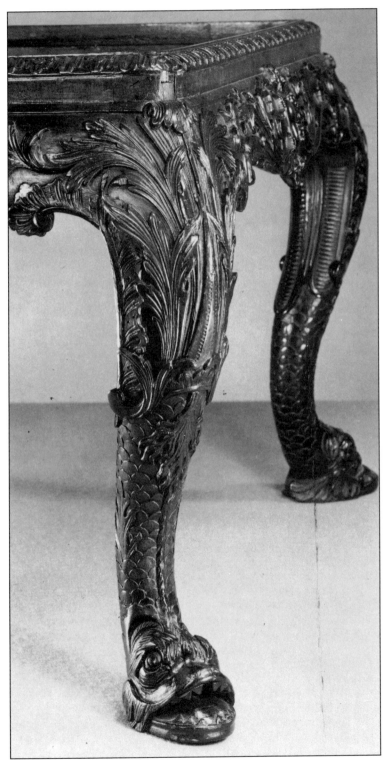

LEFT *Close-up of part of a mid-eighteenth century mahogany stool – a classic example of what can be achieved in the cabriole leg when a master carver goes to work. The leg come to life with fish motifs, head, scales and tail: a masterpiece for an opulent and elegant setting.*

BELOW *A Regency mahogany chair-stool on reeded, tapered legs. Such a piece might be found in the nursery, for use either by children or nursemaid.*

Chapter Nine

Sociable Seats

ABOVE Mme Récamier, *by J. L. David (1748-1825). Now hanging in the Louvre, Paris. David's painting of 1800 made such an impact that the chaise longue in France became known as the* récamier *in many circles.*

To help the reader through complicated terminology, this chapter must begin with a series of definitions:

Sofa: 'Long upholstered seat for two or more persons. The name "Sophia" is of eastern origin and was first used in about 1680 to designate a divan-like seat in France; the same type had also been called a *canapé*. It had a back and arms at each end, but was distinguished from the settee by its greater comfort. Sofas followed the usual evolution of the succeeding styles, varying in ornament, bulk and comfort through the styles of the eighteenth and nineteenth centuries.'

Divan: 'Upholstered couch without arms or back, originating in the Turkish form of a pile of rugs for reclining.'

Settee: 'Light open seat about twice the width of a chair, with low arms and back, sometimes upholstered.'

Couch: 'Sofa which has a half-back and head-end only.'

Day-bed: 'Rest-beds, chaise longues and other elongated seating forms may be called day-beds; these usually have a raised pillow-like end. They are pictured in ancient Greek and Roman remains and occur in France after the Louis XIV era. They appear in England with the Restoration. The commoner reference in America is to a true bed form with both ends the same height and placed lengthwise to the wall. This form grew out of the alcove bed of eighteenth-century France...'

Chaise longue: 'A long chair; a form of sofa or day-bed with upholstered back for reclining. French eighteenth century types were often made in two or three parts; the two-part type consisting of a

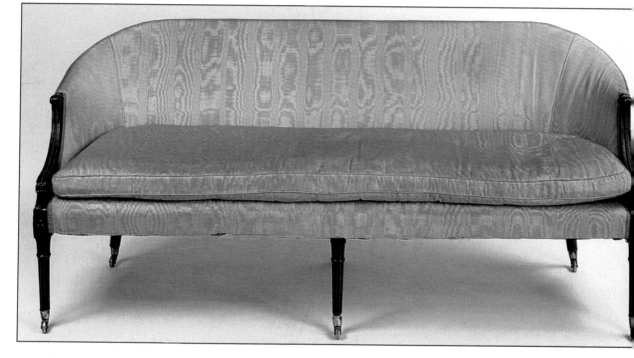

deep *bergère* and a large stool; the three-part style had two armchairs and a stool between them.'

The definitions are taken from Joseph Aronson's *Encyclopedia of Furniture*, 1938, and encountered *en masse* probably leave the reader as confused as the author admits to being. For the terminology of reclining furniture, pitted with French expressions and snared with Anglo-American variations, is a quagmire. Let us plunge into it, grasping at the term chaise longue, if only for the reason that it allows us to begin this account with the story of a beautiful woman.

The chaise longue had already existed for nearly two centuries when, in 1800, it achieved a high point in its fortunes. The historic moment came when Jacques-Louis David laid brush to canvas in his famous portrait of Madame Récamier. Jeanne Françoise Julie Adélaide Récamier was a woman of surpassing beauty and unblemished reputation, whose attractions were to last into old age

ABOVE *Clean lines and sophistication mark this carved mahogany settee of the Adam period. Tapered legs are terminated in brass cappings and castors.*

RIGHT AND BELOW RIGHT *Companions of the drawing-room: one of a pair of 'love seats', to hold two people, is shown with two of the accompanying six chairs that make up this set of George II carved mahogany seat furniture. The stuffover seats are of horsehair. Quality of carving, multiplicity of pieces and the rarity of combination joined together with their provenance – Aspley House, Bedfordshire – meant that in 1984 they fetched £22,000.*

FAR RIGHT ABOVE *A gondola-shaped giltwood chaise longue of the Louis XV period (1715-1774) demonstrates how this particular type grew out of the idea of an armchair. Pieces of furniture such as this were the vehicle for upholstery furnishings of the richest variety, and when not in use they were protected by loose covers.*

and were certainly unflawed at the age of 23 when she sat for David. Married at 15 to a wealthy banker, she exercized influence and power in Parisian literary and political circles. It was inevitable, therefore, that the official painter of the Napoleonic age should choose her as a subject. It was logical, too, that he would match her physical beauty with an exquisite piece of furniture, the chaise longue, one of the many fine items which furnished his studio.

Such was the quality and fame of David's resulting work of art, now in the Louvre Museum, that the French to this day often refer to a chaise longue as a *récamier*. Variously, as we know, it is called a rest-bed or a day-bed, and also *turquoise*, *lit de repos*, *veilleuse* and *duchesse*. By any name, it is an elegant piece of furniture designed for a leisured and mannered society. Sheraton, writing about chaises longues in his *Drawing Book*, observed in 1791: 'These have left their name from the French, which imports a long chair. Their use is to rest or loll upon after dinner.'

Sheraton told only part of the story. Having been introduced in France in about 1625, chaises longues were, by 1650, appearing in written descriptions which indicated their use for entertaining purposes and the receiving of guests. Long before the days of Madame Récamier, the queens of society received in informal attire, reclining on their chaises longues. They were expected to hide their bare feet with a coverlet of embroidered silk, a nicety dispensed with by David in the interests of art. The fine classical lines of David's studio chaise longue (its two equally-tall ends curve over with swan's-neck grace) give much to his famous picture. Similar pieces of furniture would have been found in Madame Récamier's celebrated apartments – which were planned by the leading upholsterer Berthaud and his

ABOVE *Another settee of the Adam period, in carved giltwood. The graceful lines of the cresting on the back, continued into the line of the arm supports, lend this piece a regal air.*

collaborators – for the chaise longue naturally belonged in such opulent surroundings.

The rest-beds of similar form which are pictured in Greek and Roman art were obviously used for reclining. In the first quarter of the seventeenth century, however – when such pieces of furniture appeared in France – they commonly served as seats. The earliest were made with either one or two dossiers, or ends. Legs, some six or eight, were turned and often united by carved or turned stretchers. By the days of Louis XIV (whose reign began in 1643) they were universally popular in France, while England was introduced to them under the Restoration (1660). (This development provides a further instance of the effect of the return of King Charles and his court upon furnishing and living styles in England.) Cane was a common material used in rest and day-beds during the reign of Charles II; it was often combined with walnut in an attractive style reflecting French fashion.

An important revolution in seat furniture – a marriage of luxury and comfort – took place during the latter half of the seventeenth century. This partly revealed itself with the introduction of upholstery fixed to the framework of wood, superseding the movable upholstery of cushions which had hitherto been the norm. In the France of Louis XIV costly silks and brocades were employed. These were often covered by loose drapes of less expensive materials,

LEFT *Another giltwood chaise longue of the Louis XV period shows the fullness of the upholstery and highlights the point that most reclining furniture of the eighteenth century, especially French examples, relied on the addition of a separate mattress. When using the chaise longue on social occasions, ladies would remove their shoes but conceal their feet beneath a decorative coverlet.*

BELOW *This Louis XVI (1774-1793) chaise longue is sometimes termed a* duchesse brisée. *It is composed of two distinct sections, the* bergère *which resembles a version of an armchair – and the longer section for the legs and feet of the user.*

as people, however finely dressed, tended to be rather dirty. In the great salons it was a matter of critical protocol to decide for which visitors the covers would be taken off the chairs and chaises longues. High, carved dossiers of giltwood were a feature of the rest-beds of the time, some of which were fixed to the wall.

Under Louis XV (1715-1774) the chaise longue was perfected and it appeared in a wide range of variations. There was the basic form of the chaise longue, which had a curved back like a gondola and a mattress, and was sometimes called by the French a *duchesse*. Its relationship to the sofa and the settee is close. However, there was no mistaking the uniqueness of the *duchesse brisée*, a piece of furniture broken into three or two parts. In three parts it consisted of a *bergère*, or upholstered armchair, an upholstered stool and a low *bergère* for the feet. The central upholstered stool often had concave ends which fitted neatly into the curved seat-fronts of the two *bergères*. Sometimes the *bergères* were identical, giving the impression of two facing and connected armchairs. In two parts, the *duchesse brisée* was a deep *bergère*, and a stool larger than the type found in the three-part version. In such a variety of forms the chaise longue lent itself to some interesting permutations for eighteenth-century ladies – and their lovers. Two centuries later, no amount of custom-made furniture marketing has produced a better or more comfortable vantage point for watching television!

In the Louis XVI period (1774-1793) the chaise longue continued in one, two, or three parts. But by the early nineteenth-century Empire era, created practically by edict of Napoleon, it was to be found mainly in one piece, classical in line and made of mahogany, rosewood or ebony. Upholstery in France was of hard-texture fabric, decorated with Napoleonic emblems of the crown, the bee and the letter N. In America, where the chaise longue enjoyed its happiest vogue during the Federal days, when the classic line was in

RIGHT *A Louis XVI grey painted* lit de repos *has ends of equal height, giving it the appearance of a normal bed or an alcove bed used in France in the eighteenth century. Nevertheless, this was an item of furniture for daytime use in the living room of the home, and was much in demand on social occasions.*

LEFT AND BELOW *The fact that this drawing room suite is cloaked in temporary upholstery, awaiting the designer's choice, merely highlights the elegant lines of its components. Dating from the George III period, and created in gilded wood, the suite consists of a settee and four elbow chairs, the latter with oval backs.*

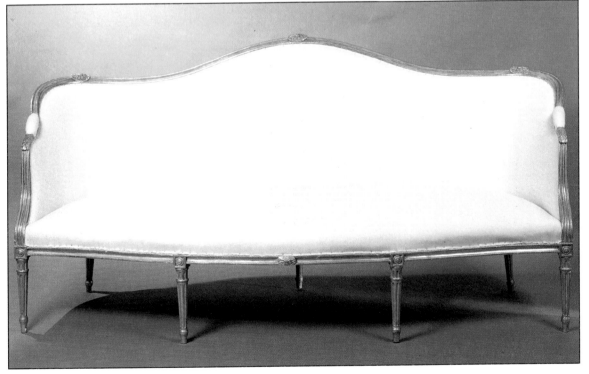

ABOVE *Age of elegance, age of leisure: Regency grace is epitomized in this day-bed, painted to resemble rosewood, with chinoiserie decoration. Its scroll end and the stool-like extension for the feet are distinctive features of an aristocratic piece of furniture.*

RIGHT *Decorative pieces such as this Chippendale-period window seat would have been scattered in large numbers in the rooms and halls of a big house in the eighteenth century. The seat, with scrolled ends, is covered in* gros point *needework and measures 4ft (1.2m) in width. The cabriole legs make much use of acanthus leaf and C-scroll carved ornament.*

harmony with the heady ideas of freedom in a new nation, the term most frequently used is that of day-bed. Often, however, as demonstrated in Aronson's definition, this refers to the truer bed style, with both ends of equal height.

In England there was a settee called a 'confidante' in the eighteenth century. Adam designed one for Sir Abraham Hume in 1780, and another is depicted in the 1788 edition of Hepplewhite's *Guide*. For two sitters who desired intimacy while at the same time preserving a modicum of isolation, the seats at either end of the settee

were separated by an upholstered barrier. These confidantes had some popular offshoots, which were often referred to as 'sociables' – groupings of two or three chairs in fixed arrangement, to be placed in the centre of a room (ideal for palm courts and exhibitions) where they would facilitate conversation; one such arrangement was a joined pair of upholstered seats whose backline formed an S-shape, allowing the sitters to converse intimately although facing in opposite directions.

Victorian England took eagerly to the chaise longue (it had long been called a couch). It represented for the aspirant, newly-rich merchant classes a link with the aristocratic. Mid-Victorian excesses added grotesque scroll-carving to back pieces. Other couches, included the popular deep buttoning, echoed in matching sets of low chairs. Neo-anything ruled – classic, gothic, Elizabethan, Jacobean, Sheraton. Sometimes over-stuffed upholstery clothed practically the entire wooden framework, apart from the turned legs, transforming the elegant chaise longue into a sausage.

After some three centuries of life the chaise longue maintained its popularity beyond the close of the First World War, through the 1920s and well into the 1930s. In Britain most working-class and lower middle-class households were not complete without their couch or wrongly termed 'sofa' (the name you gave to the piece often depended on the extent of your social aspirations). Cheap, horsehair stuffed examples were made by the hundred thousand. A typical one had a roll end, with an upholstered backrail supported on short turned columns. Turned legs were mounted on castors. In many a

ABOVE *Day-bed of the sumptuous French Empire period, known graphically as a* lit en bâteau. *Its shiplike lines are immediately obvious. Matching bolsters complement the outswept scroll ends. Ormolu reliefs, depicting mermaids and a sea goddess, decorate what is in truth a piece meant for a captain among mariners.*

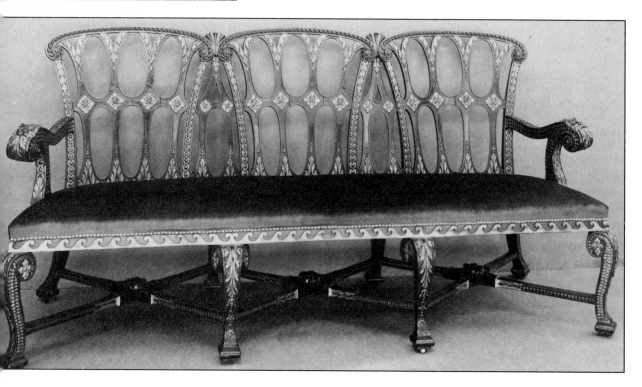

ABOVE *Enshrined in the Victoria and Albert Museum, London, is this carved and parcel-gilt mahogany settee from a set of 10 chairs and two settees formerly at Wroxton Abbey, Oxfordshire. It is attributed to William Kent and dates from about 1730-40.*

British home this humble and mass-produced descendant of the *grands salons* was as essential to furnishing as the upright piano and the large drop or draw-leaf table covered by a velvet tablecloth. Its decline was signalled by the arrival of the three-piece suite in much the same way as the 'tile-surround' fireplace, allied with centrally-heated water, condemned the magnificent combination of iron firegrate, boiler and oven, burnished to black beauty by years of hard-labour and love.

In recent years, as furnishing tastes have veered away from the three-piece suite towards individual items of seat furniture grouped together in a room, the chaise longue has once more come into its own. During the mid-1970s good Victorian chaises longues, either of straightforward nineteenth-century roll-end form or reproductions of former ages, were bargains in the antique shops at less than £100. Many have leapt more than ten times in value since then. Fine examples from the eighteenth century are as expensive as any seat furniture from that period.

Let us return to Madame Récamier. Picture the setting of her splendid apartments. Curtains of violet, black and ochre were draped in complicated fashion, each fold meticulously planned, contrived and held in place. On the walls, Beauvais tapestries depicted a pastoral France in delicate colours. Into this framework the furniture was positioned – red-brown mahogany relieved by the controlled use of citron wood and silver inlay, with no single piece having a place which was not decreed by the designers. And in central focus was the chaise longue.

From this, the beautiful Récamier dispensed a mixture of social gossip, political intrigue and personal magnetism. The first ensured her an eager and constant following. The second earned her banishment from Paris for a time. The third, allied as it was to a maddening sexual inaccessibility, brought down the displeasure of a thwarted Napoleon Bonaparte. His eye having lighted on her, the emperor sent his police commissioner, Fouché, on the pretext of inviting Récamier to be 'a lady-in-waiting to the empress'. The answer was a polite but cool refusal. Hardly a point to be found in the customary annals of furniture, yet it proved a classic case of the chaise longue dictating to the throne.

ABOVE *The superb, languorous lines of high-Regency are shown in this chaise longue of the early-nineteenth century. The woodwork is finely painted with chinoiserie scenes of pagodas and figures, with additional foliate decoration. A magnificent setting for a beautiful woman holding court in London's fashionable social circles.*

LEFT *From approximately the same era, but with smart American pedigree, comes this Federal carved mahogany sofa in the manner of Samuel McIntire of Salem, Massachusetts.*

Chapter Ten
Art Nouveau

In the collection of the Victoria and Albert Museum, London, stands an Art Nouveau chair, and companion furniture: silent testimony to the triumph of new ideas. The group of furniture is now hailed as a selection of masterpieces from the workshop of a great maker, but for fifty years it was shut away from sight, 'in disgrace'. The story starts at the 1900 Paris Exhibition. One of the exhibitors was Louis Majorelle, of Nancy, who immersed himself in the full spirit of Art Nouveau, the controversial gospel propagated throughout Europe by the disciples of William Morris. Majorelle's work in furniture embraced some of the themes which were to lead many of his compatriots into scorned excesses of decorative behaviour. Gallic enthusiasm for the organic line – epitomized in the swirling plant motif – led to many of these excesses. Daring as he was in his 'sculptured' furniture, however, Majorelle never allowed an element of vulgarity to intrude.

His chair, for example, has a frame carved in tendrils, which give it a fluidity of line, the theme being maintained in the fabric of the upholstery. But the *pièce de résistance* is a tall mahogany cabinet,

decorated with marquetry of several woods, the use of which gives it a rich effect of gently contrasting veneers and grain. The cabinet has a sturdy yet graceful plant motif framing the front. Tendrils and flowers enclose an interior sunburst design in the hooded top part of the piece. A benefactor bought the chair and cabinet, with other Majorelle items, and shipped them from the Paris exhibition to the South Kensington Museum, now the Victoria and Albert Museum. The idea was to display the collection to students as a good example of contemporary art. However, commentators of the day rose in fury and attacked Majorelle's works as 'corrupting'. So great was the opposition that the collection was withdrawn and consigned to a cellar for half a century, before claiming its righful place among recognized works of art.

Passions aroused by Majorelle's furniture would not have come as a surprise to the exponents of Art Nouveau. Even to this day, for every enthusiast there is a vilifier. In 1895 a French art critic had written of the style: 'All this seems to have the air of a vicious Englishman, the Jewess addicted to morphine, the Belgian trickster,

RIGHT *The essence of rectilinear Art Nouveau form, allied to the organic line, is epitomized in this inlaid mahogany dining chair, one of a set of 10, probably by J.S.Henry. The circular panel at the top of the back is inlaid in fruit woods with a stylized foliate and floral motif. Note the simple tapering legs standing on pad feet.*

or an agreeable salad of these poisons.' Notwithstanding the journalist's xenophobia and anti-semitism, his words echo much of the story of Art Nouveau, which has not had a simple and easy passage. Another leading French designer to be victimized for his works was Hector Guimard. He displayed a full-blooded enthusiasm for the curvilinear motif – sometimes with bizarre results according to his contemporary opponents. Should you wish to see his art in its full glory, however, you need only walk along the Parisian boulevards, where Guimard-designed entrances to Metro stations, living structures of wrought iron and glass, are a monument to him. Aversion to the new art form was so marked, particularly in the years following the First World War, that much fine furniture of the period has been destroyed: hence the scarcity and high values of quality pieces in the salerooms and specialist shops today. Inevitably, the scarcity of Art Nouveau furniture has created an international market in which British, German, French and other European dealers comb each other's countries for available pieces; and there is now a strong Japanese interest. Sets of Art Nouveau chairs are particularly keenly sought today.

To understand what happened to chairs in the Art Nouveau revolution, one must know something about the general development

LEFT *Art Nouveau touches are to be found in this rare, Bishop's triple-seated throne. The high back is decorated with a silkwork triptych of panels depicting figures in ecclesiastical scenes, notably a woman in true pre-Raphaelite style. Ivory mounting, with inset hardstone, gives the piece a rich appearance.*

of the movement. In talking of Art Nouveau, we are referring basically to a period of little more than 30 years, from the middle of the 1880s to the outbreak of the 1914-18 war. However, the ideas planted in the early days of the new style matured into functionalism which was to lead to the Modern Movement and the Bauhaus era, ushered in by Walter Gropius and his followers in 1919. Later still, the movement reaches into our architecture, with imaginative,

RIGHT *This furniture is from an unusual carved and decorated salon suite comprising a settee, three elbow and four single chairs, and a pair of centre tables. The suite has Middle Eastern overtones, and represents that part of Art Nouveau thought which turned towards the exotic. It would be a bold and unconventional furnishing scheme which found a happy home for such exotica.*

RIGHT *An ebonized 'Egyptian Revival' chair, with upholstered back and stuffover seat, making effective display of spindled back and stretchers. The shaped and tapered legs, too, are distinctive. Chairs such as this have been attributed to John Moyr; there is an alternative view which links them with E.W.Godwin.*

flowing, yet functional designs such as Eero Saarinen's TWA terminal at Kennedy Airport, New York.

Art Nouveau is an area of confusion and contradiction. The name itself is by no means universally used. Although the movement had its genesis in Britain, that country has taken the name from a shop opened in 1895 by Samuel Bing in Paris: '*La Maison de l'Art Nouveau*'. Oddly, the French do not use this name, but prefer *Le Style Moderne* or even *Style Anglais*. The Italians refer to *Style Liberty*, after the Regent Street store in London which did so much to popularise the new art among the middle and lower-middle classes of Britain. In Austria, the term is *Sezession* and the Germans say *Jugendstil*.

If we examine the background of Art Nouveau, we see how the Arts and Crafts movement of the late-nineteenth century developed from the teaching of John Ruskin, William Morris and the pre-Raphaelites, a revolt against the mass-produced machine age of the Victorians. Later, many of the exponents of the creed argued successfully for the logic of using machine mass-production to make examples of the new art available to all. Indeed, one of the principal tenets of Arts and Crafts – a loosely grouped association of artists and designers – was that quality of design and manufacture, rather than rarity or costliness of raw materials, should be the hallmark of value.

LEFT *An American Arts and Crafts oak reclining chair, in the manner of A.H.Davenport, a designer of Boston, Massachusetts. It has a leather upholstered seat and back, and reclining mechanism. The flared legs and spindle sides are particularly striking features. It bears a retail plaque, naming Easy-Poise, which was a mail-order furniture company operating between 1905 and 1920.*

Through widespread and complicated transfusion of ideas, changes in thought, experimentation with and corruption of original principles, Art Nouveau has come to mean many things to many people. The mystical semi-nude ladies, to be found in legion as statuettes, on ashtrays and inkstands and entwining themselves round mirrors, would seem to be removed from the geometrical, uncompromising seat furniture of Glasgow's Charles Rennie Mackintosh, whose cube-based forms exerted a deep influence in Austria and Germany and whose ideas blazed a trail for the Bauhaus school. As different as the two stylistic themes are, they are the twin components of Art Nouveau thinking: on the one hand, the obsession with nature – the organic art of the plant; on the other, the rectilinear, geometric idea, derived from architecture, founded in functionalism and resulting in some of the finest chair designs to emerge during the Art Nouveau period.

In an art form based on the freeing of ideas from previous shackles of thought and design, it is appropriate that the name 'Liberty' stands so high. Arthur Lazenby Liberty opened his store in

BELOW *The Egyptian flavour, by courtesy of Carlo Bugatti. This small* banquette *employs several aids to decoration, including pewter inlay, applied beaten-copper, and vellum painted with bamboo, leaves and an Arabic inscription. Again, it is something for an unconventional home: Bugatti is not to everybody's taste. Indeed, the value of Bugatti's furniture fluctuates at auction.*

Regent Street, London, in 1875, largely with a stock of goods in oriental style. The Japanese impact on furniture and other wares had begun to be felt after the opening of Japan by Commodore Perry in 1859. In the next 20 years, English furniture increasingly followed a Japanese style. Some of the notable examples were from the designs of William Godwin, architect and a close friend of the American artist James McNeill Whistler, who brought with him to England his passion for all things Japanese. Liberty was much influenced by Whistler, and Japanese style was often apparent in the flood of inexpensive, well-made goods (furniture, fabrics, silver and jewellery) which poured from his store to the public. Among the many talented designers he employed (and here we are not basically concerned with the excellent work of the silversmiths and pewterers responsible for the famous Liberty's Cymric and Tudric ware, so much as the furniture specialists) was Charles Annesley Voysey, again an architect as well as a furniture designer. Classic proportions and simplicity of structure, often incorporating tall, slender chair-backs, mark his work. Popular adaptations of his designs found a

LEFT *Dating from around 1900 is this Art Nouveau oak dining chair which makes striking use of the rising plant motif in splat and top-rail. Inlay is of pewter and ebony.*

ready market at Liberty's, as did the amended styles of Charles Rennie Mackintosh, leader of a powerful and individualistic group of designers based in Glasgow.

Mackintosh left an indelible mark on Art Nouveau design, especially in the area of furniture and particularly in chairs. No longer was the flourishing of applied art restricted to the salons and boudoirs of the rich. Appropriately, one memorial to Mackintosh is Miss Cranston's tea-rooms in Buchanan Street, Glasgow, which he designed throughout – furniture, wall decoration, silver and china. His furniture ideas were based on sound, structural common sense, owing more to a geometrical than organic origin. Traditional Art Nouveau beauties in swirling gowns, and standing amid spiralling tendrils, decorated the walls. But this decoration merely complemented the rectilinear functionalism of the furniture: chairs of splendid proportion, with high backs giving them almost an ecclesiastical look, and flat planes relieved by cut-outs. In contrast is an armchair designed for the tea-rooms in 1904 in black-stained oak with upholstered squab seat. Its flat back, sides and other surfaces and geometrical cut-outs give it a solid and square appearance.

Any study of Art Nouveau furniture is in danger of developing into a directory of names. Nevertheless, mention should be made of Selwyn Image (a splendid name for this subject!), who in 1881 founded with Arthur Mackmurdo the Century Guild, the first truly Art Nouveau guild of the Arts and Crafts movement. In their hands, nature was not merely copied, but adapted and built-upon to give furniture, and especially chairs, free-flowing vertical lines.

RIGHT *An oak chair designed by C.F.A. Voysey and made by Story and Co. in 1899.*

FAR RIGHT *An oak chair designed by Charles Rennie Mackintosh for the Glasgow School of Art, dating from about 1897.*

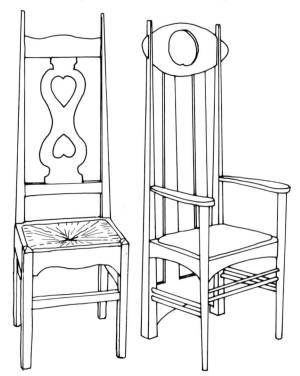

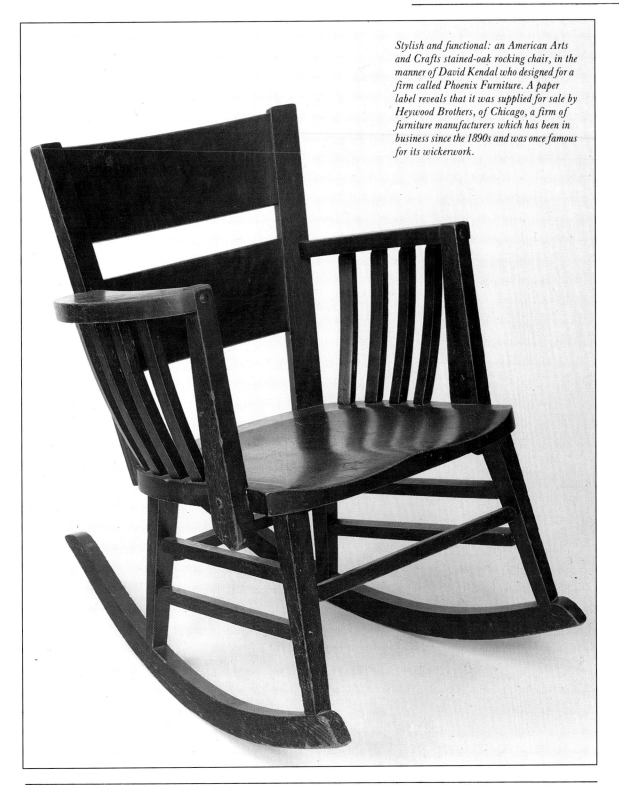

Stylish and functional: an American Arts and Crafts stained-oak rocking chair, in the manner of David Kendal who designed for a firm called Phoenix Furniture. A paper label reveals that it was supplied for sale by Heywood Brothers, of Chicago, a firm of furniture manufacturers which has been in business since the 1890s and was once famous for its wickerwork.

Chapter Eleven
Edwardian Scope

Stylish, functional, durable, borrowing the best of earlier styles, well-made...all this can be said of good Edwardian furniture. There are two other important factors, however, which have pushed Edwardian furniture forward in esteem in recent years: availability and price. It is significant that Edwardian furniture – its 'period' being, generally speaking, the better part of the first two decades of the twentieth century – has featured prominently, year in, year out, in the annual surveys of antiques at auction issued by Phillips. Based on a poll of the firm's specialists throughout the country, these surveys present a picture of trends in furniture and other items sold at auction. For several years Edwardian pieces have shown strong evidence, according to the experts, of rising demand and value.

The better pieces of Edwardian furniture find their way into the top class sales of fine furniture at several of the major auction houses.

Sets of chairs, evocative of Sheraton or the Regency period, command particularly high prices. Middle-of-the-road examples are to be found in quantities that were unknown in the late-1970s and early-1980s. Availability has much to do with this upsurge of interest. Fine quality eighteenth-century furniture has become so scarce – and correspondingly pricey – that dealers, collectors and home-furnishers have naturally looked to new areas.

Thus we saw the great move towards Victoriana. That allegiance is still holding strong, and nineteenth-century pieces which once would not have been accepted by some salerooms are now treated with reverence and given lavish catalogue illustration on both

sides of the Atlantic. For the buyer seeking elegance, however – assuming he or she cannot afford it at eighteenth-century furniture prices – Victorian is not always the answer. Its eclectic but often ponderous styles possibly may not harmonize with modern furnishing schemes and small rooms. In any case, Victorian values have already begun to leave the 'underpriced' bargain basement of furniture: witness what has happened to the once eschewed button-back seating. Hence the turn to Edwardian, a style much nearer to our own times, and one which was waiting its turn to command attention. In this field of furniture, especially when applied to chairs, style tends practically always to be retrospective, but, considering that it represents the last era in which craftsman techniques were employed on a wide scale, much of Edwardian furniture is still underpriced.

The style we now know as 'Edwardian' raided the best of

ABOVE *'Edwardian furniture', as we know it, is rising steadily in value. It seldom had an original style of its own, but borrowed much from Sheraton and from Regency. These nineteenth-century mahogany chairs are in a form much copied by the Edwardian furniture-makers.*

eighteenth-century thought in a neo-neo-classical splurge, and this theme accounts for much of its present-day popularity. Furthermore, it is still widely available. Frequently veneered in fine satinwood and with attractive inlay or marquetry, Edwardian furniture is seen at its best in elegant sets of chairs, echoing Sheraton or Regency themes (of all the masters of the past, Sheraton, was to become the most compelling single influence for Edwardian makers), glazed display cabinets, delicately fashioned writing furniture, and neat corner cupboards. Recent years have seen a quickening of values attributable in part to ever-increasing American interest: many transatlantic buyers detect in Edwardian furniture a resemblance to the grace and style of early nineteenth-century American Federal designs, particularly the chairs with their finely tapering legs and skilful inlay in the backs. It is still possible, however, to furnish a room with good pieces dating from the first decade of this century at considerably less than the cost of modern items. And like most good, old furniture, the best of Edwardian appreciates in value as the owner uses it.

Functional though the furniture is (employing mahogany for substance and satinwood for appeal), it is never clumsy. Edwardian style has a decidedly feminine quality. It belongs to the world of the 'Gibson Girl'; and despite the confines of Edward VII's reign, 1901-1910, it has more place in *fin de siècle* gaiety than in the dawning realities of the decade immediately prior to the First World War. It is a credit to the quality of Edwardian furniture that the more impressive items are now being 'saved' by the major salerooms to go into special auctions, where they rub shoulders with the true, aristocratic, period pieces of Sheraton and Regency which they directly emulate.

Edwardian chairs are represented in every form that was to be found in the decades which preceded and followed the juncture of the eighteenth and nineteenth centuries. Cane often appears as a component used to attractive effect, and some examples of moderately skillful painted satinwood exist. There are, in addition, some interesting Edwardian occasional chairs, such as tub and corner seats, which, although not providing mainstream furnishing convenience, are attractive items to have around a modern town home or a country cottage. Chairs – as this book is at pains to stress – do not stand in isolation in a home, however.

Assume, therefore, that the Edwardian convert has chosen an elegant set of dining chairs (possibly harking back to the 'Trafalgar' style of the previous century, but at a quarter of the price of the true article), an interesting collection of occasional chairs which can still be found relatively inexpensively at a general furniture dealer's shop; and perhaps, too, a few examples of comfortable Edwardian button-back chairs. What next? What other Edwardian furnishings should be sought, to harmonize with these eminently serviceable examples of seat furniture, none of which can yet be classified as antique in the literal, hundred-year, sense of the term?

Edwardian furniture is at its finest and most versatile in display cabinets, used for showing off collections of ceramics, silver or knick-

ABOVE *An illustration from a manufacturer's catalogue showing an Edwardian* bergère *chair available in either walnut or mahogany, with caned sides and back. The upholstery would have been in silk tapestry, damask or velour.*

TOP *A mahogany, fireside armchair; the seat would have been covered in either silk tapestry or damask.*

knacks. The Edwardian householder wanted space, airiness and visibility: therefore Edwardian display cabinets are not cluttered with an excessive burden of woodwork on their glazed fronts. The glass is framed in delicate tracery; and the contents are shown to extremely good effect.

Edwardian writing furniture excels in small, attractive pieces designed for the lady of the house to use in her boudoir, in emulation of her forebears of Regency times or even earlier. Today these small desks and writing tables have come out into the general living rooms of the house, a happy complement to the range of Edwardian occasional chairs. D-ended dining tables of mahogany and rosewood, crafted in the decade prior to the 1914-18 war, do splendid service in homes which could not possibly afford a Regency version. Occasional tables, enhanced by modest marquetry decoration or boxwood stringing, abound, and represent some of the best bargains to be found in Edwardian furniture.

The 1970s and 1980s have seen an enormous advance in the appreciation of Edwardian furniture. The road has not been altogether easy, however. Here is the author's good friend, David Moss, a former editor of the sadly missed magazine, *Art & Antiques Weekly*, writing in 1972, as the public began to think tentatively of 'buying Edwardian':

'The pieces which are making an impact in the auction houses

BELOW *More Regency chairs which found ready echoes in the Edwardian period: mahogany diners with rope-twist decoration in the backs. In the Regency version (shown here), a set of six in 1989 have fetched £10,000-£12,000 at auction. Edwardian examples fetch about a third of that price.*

and creeping into the showrooms at the moment are the Edwardian "copies" of eighteenth-century styles. These are controversial in the sense that at a glance one can tell they are vastly inferior to eighteenth-century work. But they do not purport to be anything more than copies, and with the prohibitive price of eighteenth-century furniture it seems inevitable that this popular "Edwardian" line would inevitably appeal to the public – who are, after all, the final, arbiters of a piece's acceptability, if not its status.'

He quotes H. Avery Tipping, a furniture authority opining in *Country Life* in 1909: 'Copying takes us no further. Its adoption as a system is a sign of arrested development of an age that is tired and will shortly decay.' Then, David Moss continues:

'I take Mr Tipping's point. It does bring out the fact that the Edwardians did not achieve a style of their own. But with rapid industrialization and the onset of the more unpleasant traits of modern marketing, I can understand those Edwardians who preferred earlier, stable, reassuring lines when they came to furnish their homes. Like us, they could not afford the real thing.

'Sheraton, Chippendale, Adam and Hepplewhite's styles were all resurrected. Many Regency pieces were also reproduced. But although they are copies they are unmistakably Edwardian. Without doubt there was appreciation and enthusiasm for the furniture of the eighteenth-century, but there was also a misunderstanding of style and technique.' Here, he quotes Alan Rubin, a furniture specialist then working for Phillips: 'The quality was often very good but there were misconceptions. But there was never any attempt to deceive. The colour is generally wrong and there are also mistakes in proportion. This was bound to happen because Edwardian craftsmen were not capable of accurately seeing the eighteenth-century way of doing things.' Having acknowledged the drawbacks of Edwardian furniture, however, Messrs Rubin and Moss were aware of its attributes and its undoubtedly rosy prospects in the modern market.

ABOVE *An Edwardian tub-shaped, drawing-room chair of inlaid mahogany, in a style reminiscent of an earlier age.*

BELOW *Another Regency style that was to be copied nearly a century later. Good, solid rail-back chairs, to grace any dining room.*

Mr Moss detected an ever-increasing interest in Edwardian furniture. He wrote: 'One can find quality in the early- twentieth century. If you can afford eighteenth-century furniture you can afford to snigger at the best Edwardian. But a rapidly increasing number of people cannot.'

In those distant days of the early 1970s he discovered a leading and far-sighted auctioneer who predicted the day would come when salerooms would devote special auctions to Edwardian furniture. For its time, it seemed a bold and optimistic forecast. But the projected scenario has come to pass. Moreover, as the popularity of Edwardian furniture has brought to light increasingly numerous examples of good craftsmanship, the period has successfully shed its reputation as merely a second-class, hit-and-miss copy of past glories. Many pieces do reveal erratic attempts at interpretation, but an unexpectedly large quantity of fine examples of the joiner and cabinetmaker's art have been uncovered. Happily, commonsense and market forces have been able to sort out the sheep from the goats. Today, Edwardian chairs, tables and cabinets enhance many a tasteful furnishing scheme.

ABOVE *Typical Edwardian furniture which would have been part of a seven-piece couch suite, incorporating two armchairs, four dining chairs and a full-length couch.*

Chapter Twelve
Country Seats

ABOVE *The all-conquering Windsor chair was traditionally the result of a 'co-operative' chain of craftsmen, each one contributing his part to the process which facilitated the progress of the chair from the beechwoods around High Wycombe in Buckinghamshire, possibly through the marketing centre of Windsor (from which the name may have been derived), to London. No chair looks more splendid in quantity: here is a set of nineteenth-century elm veterans, attractively decorated with wheel splats.*

A vintage English music-hall song goes like this:

I'm Jurkins of Wycombe, High Wycombe in Bucks.,
Where I lives with mi' wife and mi' fowls and mi' ducks,
And I turns up the spindles and makes all your chairs.
Aye! I guess I'm the man at the seat of affairs,
And whether you're high born, or proud as can be,
You'd look very low if it wasn't for me!'

Apart from Mr Jurkins, many people have been singing the praises of chairs from High Wycombe in Buckinghamshire – especially that quintessentially English, much copied, ever popular seat, the Windsor chair – for the better part of three centuries. There is a story which goes the rounds of furniture legend concerning George III; he is said to have been compelled, while taking shelter in a cottage near Windsor when hunting, to sit in a certain type of locally made chair until a thunderstorm eased off. He found his seat so comfortable that he afterwards ordered some of the chairs to be made for the royal household and named them Windsor chairs. Alas, good as the story is, Windsors were well established long before that particular George was old enough to sit in a chair, and were being advertised in the town's name before he was born.

George II paid £4 for 'a very neat mahogany Windsor chair'. Thomas Jefferson ordered a set in black and gold (painted Windsors were a popular furnishing theme), and Benjamin Franklin possessed two dozen in white – which may have meant simply unpainted ones. Although categorized now as country chairs, Windsors were given a metropolitan accolade as long ago as 1730 when a certain John Brown advertised the manufacture of 'all sorts of Windsor Garden Chairs, of all sizes, painted green or in the wood' at his furniture shop under the sign of 'the Three Cover'd Chairs and Walnut-tree in St Paul's church yard', London.

That voluble and valuable chronicler of furnishing fashion, J.C. Loudon, had something to say about Windsors in his *Encyclopedia of Cottage, Farmhouse and Villa Architecture and Furniture* in 1833. First, his comments on chair taste in general: 'Ask any cabinet-maker, and he will tell you at once that his customers prefer the ornamented chair, and care nothing about the unity, or the want of unity, or style. Their great object is to get a display of rich workmanship, at as cheap a rate as possible. Our readers, we are sure, will agree with us that this taste on the part of the purchaser is of a vulgar and grovelling kind, and ought to be corrected.'

Loudon had the answer at the tip of his quill pen; Windsors, he avowed, were the best kitchen chairs in general use. His writings have left us some chemistry secrets of the chairmaker: 'These chairs are sometimes painted, but more frequently stained in diluted sulphuric acid and logwood [dye extracted from the heart of a tree]; or by repeatedly washing them over with alum water, which has some tartar in it; they should afterwards be washed over several times with an extract of Brazil wood. The colour given will be a sort of red, not unlike that of mahogany; and, by afterwards oiling the chair and rubbing it well, and for a long time, with woollen cloths, the veins and shading of the elm will be rendered conspicuous. Quicklime slacked in urine, and laid on the wood when hot, will also stain it a red colour; and this is said to be the general practice with the Windsor chair manufacturers in the neighbourhood of London.'

Loudon's digression is useful to show how steeped in country crafts and methods was the production of Windsor chairs, probably the most available and therefore the most collectable item of old furniture on both sides of the Atlantic. Windsors came into use in England by the end of the seventeenth century, but were certainly widespread by the early-eighteenth, and have lasted and are made until this day. Their connection with the town of Windsor is, to say the least, tenuous. Possibly the Thameside town was a useful distributing or marketing point for London, but the home of the true Windsor was in the beechwoods around High Wycombe, some 13 miles away from Windsor.

There, ample supplies of beech were available for the spindles

ABOVE *Royal Windsors: one of a fine set of four George III yew and fruitwood elbow Windsor chairs 'in the Hepplewhite taste', the latter showing in the swept-back arm supports and the harmony of the cabriole legs. A top-quality set of country-style furniture, sold for £5,000 in the late 1970s, but today would fetch much more.*

in the backs, for the legs (turned or cabriole), and for the stretchers. Daniel Defoe, writing in 1725, was aware of 'a vast quantity of Beechwood which grows in the woods of Buckinghamshire more plentifully than in any other part of England'; these forests provided 'beech quarters for divers uses, particularly chair-making and turnery wares'. Traditionally, elm formed the seat which was carved into a saddle shape, and is extremely comfortable despite its solidity.

As the chair's popularity increased, it was made in several variations for the better-off homes as well as for country customers. In the more expensive chairs yew – the wood from which the great English long-bow was made – replaced beech or ash. Willow, mahogany and walnut have all been employed in the search for variety. Incidentally, beech, being a soft wood, .is susceptible to worm, so any beechwood furniture should be checked carefully for the tell-tale holes.

The hoop-back chair is the most common form of Windsor to be found in present-day antique shops. This is a style which tends to date the chair to the second half of the eighteenth century. Earlier, the English Windsor was normally the comb-back, in which the upright spindles of the back were united at the top by a horizontal crosspiece, sometimes lightly decorated with carving. To add to the collector's

BELOW RIGHT *Made for a country chapel – at Stonor Park in Oxfordshire – but showing the hand of a master: this is one of a set of four black-painted and gilt gothic-revival chairs dating from about 1765. A collector's item rather than an essential for furnishing in the present day.*

BELOW *Beech, in plentiful supply, has always been a popular wood for country chair-makers, in France as well as in England. This beech chair, with nicely-turned legs, is in the style of the Louis XV period (1643-1715).*

difficulties in dating, however, this style was often followed on both sides of the Atlantic much later than 1750. Splats varied from the simple pierced types to those embodying a wheel design, the hallmark of the highly-desirable wheel-back. In practically all the armchair Windsors there is a horizontal rail, at mid-back level, which curves round and is prolonged to form the arms, themselves supported by short spindles which could be simple dowels, heavily turned or carved to suit the maker's inclinations or his customer's pocket. Harmonious curves sometimes went into the making of the stretchers, one of the most sought-after types being the cowhorn, sometimes termed 'crinoline' in English furniture catalogues.

Basically three roles were played by the Windsor chair craftsmen. There was first the bodger, an old English term for the turner who would work in the woods, often living in a makeshift hut of brushwood and bracken, producing the spindles, legs and stretchers, which were then sent to the town. There, the bottomer fashioned the saddle seats and the remaining parts of the chair. Finally it was for the framer to assemble all the finished pieces; he used no screws or nails, no mortise-and-tenon joints, no dovetails, but simply wedged the members into the appropriate holes. Into the tripartite production line other specialists intervened to play supporting but important roles: a bender would steam and force into shape the bows, and a benchman would saw and fret the splats in the back of the chair.

Tools were practical and simple and changed little over the centuries: the bodger used a hammer-like beetle and a wedge for splitting the sawn tree trunks into billets of wood; legs were initially shaped with a spokeshave and then finished on a pole lathe; the bottomer sculpted the seats first with an adze and finished them with a travisher, which was a form of spokeshave. The swing of the adze could be dangerous to the craftsman's foot, and in High Wycombe lore there is talk of a particularly unfortunate bottomer called Billy 'No-Toes' Neville.

The Windsor chair industry recorded some impressive production statistics. By the middle of the nineteenth century there were 150 furniture factories in the High Wycombe area, making about 5,000 chairs every day. Most of the output was basic seating for homes, clubs and assembly rooms. Orders were immense: some 19,000 for a giant evangelical meeting, 8,000 for the Crystal Palace, 4,000 for St Paul's Cathedral. And as the industry extended, ancillary trades such as caning and rushing began to thrive; these normally employed women and girls at low rates of pay. A traditional local song warns the young men of High Wycombe to be wary of talking to these 'pretty caning girls', who 'steal away your heart' and then bolt with the 'blooming polishers'.

From the start of the nineteenth century salesmen with horse-drawn 'chair vans' from High Wycombe travelled round the country selling chairs and booking orders. It was common for them to fill up odd corners of their vans with lace made by local women, who were adept at this craft, and at least one of these travellers, Benjamin North, was so successful that in the 1860s he quit the road and set up

BELOW *Rustic, sturdy and desirable: an eighteeth-century yew elbow chair of a type now fetching high prices in the saleroom. Its dominant item of construction/decoration, the diagonal lattice-work, is the main attraction and the principal feature which stamps it as the product of a country workshop. Such pieces could be picked up 'for a song' in the early 1970s. Now they are given special attention as the steeply rising price of 'town' furniture fuels the search for an available alternative.*

shop in High Wycombe as 'chair manufacturer and haberdasher'. At about this time, the travelling salesmen began to carry around with them illustrated catalogues from which householders on their routes could order chairs.

When the eighteenth-century taste for the cabriole leg was interpreted in the Windsor, some makers embellished the knees with acanthus-leaf carving and other restrained decoration. These higher-quality chairs, usually of mahogany, tend to come from town and city sources, rather than the factories of the country makers. Elsewhere, there were regional variations. Windsors were also made in Yorkshire, Lancashire, Scotland and Wales. Examples from the north of England are traditionally in yew wood. What price do you pay for a Windsor? The question is not easy to answer because of the enormous variations in quality and style. Armchairs, on the whole, are worth twice as much as those chairs without arms. At the top end of the price scale are writing-arm Windsors, worth several thousand pounds apiece. The writing-arm is peculiarly American; it employs a flat writing surface on the sitter's right. Rockers, too, are probably more common in America, although they appear from time to time in English country shops; a desirable combination is a full-size rocker, with a child-sized companion chair.

The chapters on oak have looked at the history of and market forces governing some country furniture. These days, unlike the scene 30 years ago, good sets of country chairs are sure of a wholehearted and positive response when they appear in metropolitan salerooms. Happily, they are fetching equally high prices when they come up for sale in the regions of their origin; regional collectors who 'buy back their own' heritage have become a parochial as well as an international phenomenon on the saleroom front. It is a good sign, for much worthwhile furniture has been produced by country craftsmen, both designing to their own styles and interpreting the design books and dictionaries of the London cabinet-making luminaries. Yew, pine and beech and the other country woods are in demand, and chairs made from these materials seem to have a following that cannot be wholly explained by the spread of the country cottage habit or the move towards Scandinavian or 'natural' furnishing.

One region's home-produced furniture is quite likely to pop up at auction or in antique shops across the other side of the country. Yorkshire chairs find a home as readily in London as in Harrogate. Similar types, with open, arcaded backs and two crescent-shaped crossrails, manufactured in the late-eighteenth century in East Anglia or the Midlands of England, would be as eagerly bought in Scotland or in Wales as in their areas of origin.

When the author approached dealers and auction house specialists in various parts of the country, enquiring about the elements they favoured, many replies stressed the importance of quality. Run-of-the-mill country chairs, and particularly singles, do not attract much attention; buyers seek good craftsmanship and *sets* of chairs: this seemed to be the message of the author's 'market survey'.

BELOW *A Windsor rarity: one of a set of four George III yew chairs in the gothic style. The type of stretcher is known as crinoline.*

In Hertfordshire, a dealer in English domestic oak and country furniture believed that finding the goods of the right quality was the most difficult aspect of buying and selling country chairs. 'A dealer may be offered chairs daily, but the good examples are few and far between. Country chairs are in demand, but the serious buyers have a discerning eye; they are much more educated to the fine heritage which we have in furniture.' In the West Midlands an auctioneer said: 'Country chairs must be attractive looking and come in sets. Many dealers are not prepared to look at them unless they have that something extra – a feature which lifts them out of the ordinary. For instance, there is no trouble at all in moving a nice set of elm ladder or spindle-backs in good shape. From the Midlands sets such as these would find a ready market with dealers who want them for the Cotswolds.' He remembered handling an oak shepherd's chair, probably originating from the Midlands in the eighteenth century. It was high-backed, panelled, with a drawer under the seat in which the shepherd stored his lamb skins. Such an unusual feature immediately puts a premium on the value. Although somewhat crudely made, such an oddity can soar well into four figures at auction.

In Sussex, there was a qualified response to enquiries about the fortunes of settle-type furniture. Shepherd's chairs and others with a gimmick were fair game, but large settles were slow-sellers. An exception would be a seventeenth-century oak, box-seat settle, measuring no more than 90cm (36in) in width. Yew wood sells well,

BELOW *Variations on the Windsor. The chairs on the left and right are interesting in that they belong to a nineteenth-century harlequin, or variegated, set in which each one slightly differs from its fellows. The central chair, also Victorian, has an unusual radiating spindle splat. All are in yew and elm and sport crinoline stretchers.*

an unusual example being an eighteenth-century yew elbow chair, with trellis back almost reminiscent of a Chinese style.

In Suffolk, it was pointed out that it could be more costly to have a missing reproduction member of a set made up to order than to buy the rest of the set. Here and there, specialist joiners are kept busy filling in these gaps to special order, an operation which can be costly for the buyer after his original outlay on, say, five chairs at auction. (One reason why sets of chairs – or sets of anything for that matter – become sundered is family division of assets after a bereavement.) The Suffolk view continued: 'The demand for country chairs has become very strong. There are not enough good examples about, but for all that they still tend to be underpriced when compared to the money asked for modern furniture. Nevertheless the market is buoyant. After all, chairs are not a luxury: we all need chairs. Even if such items as credence tables fall off in demand, people will still go on buying chairs.' The source named as ready sellers groups of harlequin elbow Windsors, Lancashire spindle-backs and similar enduring products of the country workshops of the eighteenth and early-nineteenth centuries.

At Leeds there was regret over the shortage of really good sets of country chairs: 'I believe so many have been bought by overseas buyers and have left the country. The really roughly-made country furniture stays in the villages – few would want it, anyway – and there is a dearth of better-quality sets of Yorkshire and Lancashire chairs. Ladder-backs are rare.' In Bath, country fortunes were linked to the shortage of metropolitan fine pieces: 'Good provincial furniture makes high prices; just look at some of the sensational levels reached by Windsor chairs. Whether other country chairs are underpriced is a different matter. We believe country furniture has received its due recognition after being neglected for years. Of course, part of the story is the shortage of high-quality, definable London pieces from the great age of furniture; as always, people start to look for a more available alternative at a lower price. In chairs, even the lesser, Edwardian pieces find a brisk shipping outlet to the United States.'

An Edinburgh auctioneer commented: 'Country furniture underpriced? Well, it's been doing very nicely here – all varieties, in all price ranges. It is often very difficult to define regional furniture – a signed Windsor chair, for example, is a rarity, but it does crop up now and again. Scottish furniture is particularly difficult to define, but there are certain types which are readily identifiable and therefore command high prices. An example is the simple, country chair from the Orkney Islands, dating from about 1850 onwards. It is high-backed, and this part of the chair is characterized by a circle of rush. The rest is usually pine, and the seat is a plain, flat wooden one. Chairs like these have shot up in price, although the Orkneys were full of them, and a modern version is made to this day.'

One authority plotted the fortunes of a set of eighteenth-century spindle-back country chairs, region unspecified; the set consisted of six ordinary and two arm chairs. In 1971 the value was estimated to be £150-£200 for the group; in 1981, £1,500-£2,400; in 1986, £2,600-£3,200. Country seats have an interesting future.

Despite the inventive transatlantic embellishments, the Windsor chair remains an essentially English attribute. America has much fine country furniture of its own, however, and none of it better than the serenely simple genre which has brought international renown to the religious sect called the Shakers. The name 'Shaker' or 'Shaking Quaker' was first given in ridicule to members of the United Society of Believers in Christ's Second Coming because of their dramatically emotional movements during religious services. They grew from a handful of people who left England in the late-eighteenth century and initially established communities in country areas of

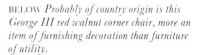

BELOW *Probably of country origin is this George III red walnut corner chair, more an item of furnishing decoration than furniture of utility.*

New York state. Later they spread to various parts of New England and as far afield as Ohio, Indiana and Kentucky. Today the sect has almost died out but their furniture lives on. Their religious beliefs, eschewing costliness and extravagance, led to a purity of form which is the basis of their designs. At a Philadelphia centennial exhibition in 1876, Shaker chairs were awarded a medal for their 'Strength, Sprightliness and Modest Beauty'. Chair backs usually have three slats slightly curved for comfort, and the legs and posts are delicately slender. Most chairs from Shaker workshops were painted – sometimes with cinnamon or tawny colours, or with thinned-down paint or varnish to allow the wood's configurations to come through. Distinctive chair patterns and styles of cabinet furniture have made Shaker furniture extremely popular, and it is today recognized as being amongst the best of modern furniture.

ABOVE LEFT *A fine example of an early Windsor chair from a collection owned by the Queen's Head, Milborne Port, Sherborne, Dorset.*

Chapter Thirteen
Modern Days

Modern furniture has its roots in the past, so we must move back into the nineteenth century to study designs which influenced twentieth-century chair-makers. Isabelle Anscombe, in the magazine *Collectors Guide*, July 1982, wrote: "'Art furniture' was a term coined in the latter half of the nineteenth century. It encompassed a wide range of influences, from the sub-gothic of Charles Eastlake, first presented to the public in 1865 in a series of articles called "Hints on Household Taste" in *The Queen* magazine, to the revolutionary Anglo-Japanese designs of E.W. Godwin. Art furniture held court in the middle-class drawing room with William Morris chintzes, illustrated books by

Kate Greenaway, Oscar Wilde's favourite blue and white china, Japanese fans, peacock feathers, lilies and sunflower motifs. Even the ladies who inhabited these rooms wore high-waisted dresses in "demure art colours".'

From Morris and Co. – founded in 1861 in response to Morris's own quest for suitable furniture which he could enjoy – came the Sussex chair, produced by the Oxford Street, London, company in many varieties. Morris's biographer, J.W. Mackail, has written: 'Of all the specific minor improvements in common household objects due to Morris, the rush-bottomed Sussex chair perhaps takes the first place. It was not his own invention, but was copied with trifling improvements from an old chair of village manufacture picked up in Sussex. With or without modification it has been taken up by all the modern furniture manufacturers, and is in almost universal use. But the Morris patterns of the later type (there were two) still excel all others in simplicity and elegance of proportion.' The Sussex chair was one of the earliest stock items produced by the Morris firm, and it continued to be a good seller into the early years of the present century. Modern furniture would learn much from this chair.

Harmony was the essence of the Sussex chair, derived, as we have seen, from the honest lines of country furniture. The chairs have a graceful, upright appearance. Contemporary catalogues show several variations, each painted black and presumably of deal. There was a plain, single chair, with rounded front legs and an interesting combination of horizontal, undecorated splats, and turned upright splats. A corner version gave the sitter ample room, not a facility usually found in this type of esoteric, triangular seating. The 'Rossetti' armchair was an elegant construction with an attractive arrangement of vertical, waisted uprights in the back, nipping in and bunching out like a sheaf of corn (or a woman's waist). A 1.3m (4ft 6in) settee, its three-piece seat made of rush and providing plenty of room, and round-seated chairs were other variations.

The Japanese vogue of the late-nineteenth century was epitomized in the abode of the painter J.M. Whistler, whose entire Chelsea home was designed in this oriental style by the architect E.W. Godwin. He demonstrated an architectural ingenuity in the design of chair legs and the stretchers which united them. At the same time, however, like Morris's designers, he strove to emulate the best that was to be found in traditional country chairs.

In 1875 Arthur Lasenby Liberty founded Liberty & Co., based in the London department store which was to become world renowned for bringing the fruits of the Arts movement to a wider middle-class public. The rules of the market were widely drawn: they allowed for a rich repertoire of design – the country-style, Japanese, Egyptian, neo-gothic, medieval, Elizabethan. Each had its fling, but by the turn of the century 'honesty' of design, materials and construction reigned supreme, in chairs as much as in all other branches of furniture and furnishings.

One designer who was faithful to the original tenets of Morris was Ernest Gimson, architect and designer, noted for his turned ash chairs with rush seats. One authority has written of him: 'His

LEFT *Part of a Gordon Russell dining room suite of furniture, fashioned in walnut with yew crossbanding. The eight chairs, including two carvers or elbow chairs, sport chamfered lattice backs, an appealing 'country' feature from the Cotswolds of England; the seats are of pigskin. The suite also includes an extending dining table, sideboard and small serving table. A typical Russell touch was the inclusion of a walnut cigar-box of hexagonal shape and en suite. In 1988 the ensemble sold at auction for £13,750.*

furniture reveals an intimate appreciation of materials and techniques (e.g. wood treated to make the most of its grain); it is elegant, clean-lined, sometimes rather spindly; often decorated with inlays and anything but cottagey.' In the early 1890s, with the brothers Sidney and Ernest Barnsley, he founded Kenton & Co for the manufacture of plain oak furniture. Then, in 1895, Gimson and the brothers set up a workshop in the Cotswolds. In 1901 Gimson employed Peter Waals to head his workshops, and he too designed simple chairs, which developed by the 1920s into plain-wood types with semi-circular slatted backs.

RIGHT *A 1960s wood and metal laminated reversible chair designed by Charles Zublena. It functions as a rocker in one position and as an armchair when reversed. The chair was purchased new in Paris in 1968, the year in which the prototype was shown at an exhibition, 'L'Art de Vivre', at the Grand Palais. A decade later it changed hands at auction for £300.*

The Cotswold connection involves Charles Robert Ashbee, architect, designer, writer and leader of the Arts and Crafts Movement. Having founded in 1888 the Guild and School of Handicraft in the East End of London, where he designed chairs and other furniture in a lighter version of the Morris style, he moved the enterprise in 1902 to Chipping Campden in the Cotswolds; there he established the School of Arts and Crafts (1904-14) which attempted to revive handicrafts and husbandry.

About a year after Ashbee arrived in Chipping Campden, an 11-year-old boy went to school in the picturesque Cotswold town, which was becoming a centre of the new applied arts. He was Gordon Russell (1892-1980). A Cotswolds son, pupil and mentor, Sir Gordon

Russell has left a reputation in furniture design spanning more than 60 years. His creations of the 1920s and 1930s became collectors' items in their own time. They attract strong bidding when they appear in the saleroom. Awards and honours were poured on the man who, while introducing new shapes in furnishings, had to contend with handwork purists who saw treason in his belief that hands and machines should be allies not foes. Russell was deeply influenced by the Cotswolds movement and when he returned from the 1914-18 war with a wound, the Military Cross, and a desire to 'set up a workshop to make decent furniture for ordinary people', the path was laid for one of the most brilliant furniture designers of our age. The rest – wartime Utility, the Council of Industrial Design, growing international renown through the products of the family firm which still bears his name in the Cotswolds – is history.

His chairs have both a strong visual attraction – forms are rectilinear, in harmonious proportions, and the patina and colour of woods such as elm and yew are exploited to the full – and the blessing of comfort: Gordon Russell could not abide an uncomfortable chair and he was loud in his praise of the dear, traditional, everlasting Windsor in this respect.

This book's principal purpose is to be a guide to the seat furniture of former centuries, to lead the reader through the pleasures and traps of the 'antique' market. Within that purpose it is relevant to review, albeit briefly, some outlines of twentieth-century chair design. Nevertheless, such a review could not be comprehensive within the confines of these pages, and much of the production of twentieth century furniture-makers requires an assessment from an historical perspective. The twentieth century, however, affords an opportunity which past times patently do not for first-hand source material. (If only we could interview Chippendale, Hepplewhite and Sheraton!) In 1978, only two years before Sir Gordon Russell's death, the author was privileged to interview the Cotswold master furniture designer at his home, for *House & Garden* magazine. What Sir Gordon had to say holds much relevance for students of furniture design, and the author here recalls that meeting in a personal account.

The Cotswolds, sweeping on in ordered folds like a well-planned extension to the garden, looked their best in the autumnal sunshine. A single robin fussed merrily at our feet. The wine was chilled to perfection and Sir Gordon Russell, 86 years of age and as lively as the robin, expounded his views on furniture design, ranging deftly from a eulogy of the eighteenth-century masters to abrasive criticism of some modern teaching techniques, from the benefits and drawbacks of wartime Utility furniture to the evils of bureaucratic meddling, and ending the interview with a brisk tour of his Chipping Campden home to point out the very latest of his furniture creations, designed at an age when lesser men's concern with furniture has narrowed to the rocking chair.

Sir Gordon beamed through his round spectacles with almost schoolboyish delight when I told him that a friend still had a much-admired nest of three tables bought at Heal's in London during the war, a product of the Russell-guided utility scheme. 'It always pleases

ABOVE *Lloyd Loom chairs, which became popular in Victorian times for use in tea-rooms and conservatories, are currently enjoying a revival to coincide with renewed interest in the conservatory. Original examples are now much sought-after.*

me when people tell me that', he said, delightedly.

I had come to Chipping Campden to talk to him shortly before he was due to address the Royal Designers for Industry on the subject of 'skill', a quality hugely apparent in a series of his latest furniture creations which he was about to 'unveil' publicly at the gathering. There was added topicality in our meeting, for only the same week furniture of the 1930s had made saleroom records when pieces of Peter Waals, the Cotswold School foreman of Gimson, fetched prices of over £2,000 at a Wiltshire auction.

Despite Sir Gordon's characteristically precise directions over the telephone, it was not difficult to get lost in the winding Cotswold lanes, but then his home suddenly became identifiable by a fleeting view of a garden with the yellow-pink landmark of a folly, a soaring fragment of a pseudo-medieval castle he has built. 'It has been 10 years in the making, and it is not yet finished', he explained. 'There are 30 steps to the top [which was surmounted by a huge Union Jack], a secret passage to the foot of the wall below and a dungeon with a place to cook bacon and eggs. The children love it.'

Before entering the house for a conducted tour to show his latest furniture designs, he talked about a remarkable supply of raw material which was offered to him constantly by friends and neighbours. 'There's elm, for instance. We've lost nearly 20 elm trees here from Dutch elm disease. A terrible blow. Then an estate manager had to fell a magnificent yew tree. A seventeenth-century

BELOW *The furniture of Gordon Russell, especially that in the Cotswold Arts and Crafts tradition, is highly regarded. From 1925 he turned to furniture of greater simplicity, some of which is seen in this view of the Russell room in the British Pavilion at the Paris Exhibition of 1937. Several Russell chairs are shown. Russell, later the high priest of wartime Utility furniture, produced some of the finest dining-room suites of the Thirties.*

house had been built too near to the tree and the roots were causing trouble in the foundations. It was offered to me, and cut into planks. I thought I'd make a dining table of yew, and a set of chairs. People ring me up and say, "I've got 50 laburnums planted at the turn of the century. Can you use them?"'

In his 'retirement' Sir Gordon had turned his designing talents to the requirements of a special client. Were his latest furniture designs for commercial purposes? He laughed: 'No. Nobody's seen them yet.' His wife, Toni, added with triumph in her voice: '*I'm* getting them. I've been waiting a long time.' And so the remains of the grand old yew tree, the bane of a seventeenth-century mansion, had pride of place in the Russells' dining room. 'An exercise in jointing,' he called it – which is the essence of much of his prize-winning furniture, especially the chairs.

Sir Gordon praised the work of the traditional High Wycombe makers of Windsor chairs, the only existing range 'slotted in' to the wartime Utility framework because of its economical and practical qualities. 'If you've got ham bones near to the surface like me', he said, 'there's nothing for comfort like the beautifully shaped elm seat of an eighteenth-century wheel-back Windsor.' Practicality was important. He went on: 'Today the modern movement has run into the sand. They are all trying to evolve shapes which have never been seen before. Chairs for instance. The result is you can't sit on them. Students could learn more by paying attention to what has been done before. After all, if you've got a thousand years of tradition, you don't want to throw it into the ditch.'

Many of Sir Gordon's most recent designs, mixed in his house with earlier examples and carefully chosen antiques, had been made up into furniture pieces by a retired manager from Gordon Russell Limited (now Gordon Russell plc), the family firm at Broadway, some three miles away. 'He had packed up his tools for 20 years, but we went to work together on odds and ends. I love experimenting', said Sir Gordon.

Although the economically-planned wartime Utility scheme, of which he was the prime architect, laid down irradicable lines of good design, beneficially affecting the course of furniture for several decades, and was a resounding success in its context, Sir Gordon was against government direction of taste in principle. (Once must recall that we were talking in 1978.) However, he just as firmly believed that people should be educated out of the old ways of accepting 'caricatures' of past styles; the 'Chippendale' cocktail cabinet in laminated plastic, the out-of-context and badly crafted mock Louis *fauteuil* – 'the first buys of the pools winner' – were a favourite target of his scorn.

Had he been born 150 years earlier, before furniture's golden age had run into Victorian sands (notwithstanding the good parts of the Victorian contribution), what role would he have filled by choice? Without hesitation, he said: 'I would have liked a small country workshop, while still occasionally spending a bit of time in London – a great furniture centre, after all. Just 12 or 20 people.' What sort of product would his country workshop have produced? His answer

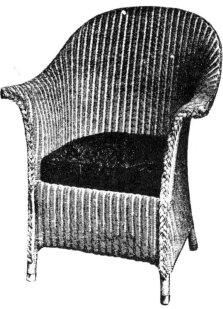

ABOVE *Two examples of the Lloyd Loom chair showing its 'moulded' shape. This type of chair was popular on both sides of the Atlantic.*

would stand as his epitaph: 'I'm all in favour of an elegance that's going out of life.'

In the opinion of Peter Philp, the distinguished and prolific writer on furniture (discoursing on styles between the wars in *Collectors Guide*, August 1988), 'of all the English designers at that time it was Sir Gordon Russell who, it seems to me, exerted the most widespread and beneficent influence'. Mr Philp pointed out that Russell was, in addition to being strong in allegiance to the English heritage, interested in the new Scandinavian school of design, and both in the Cotswolds and in London he displayed the products of Artek, the Helsinki firm founded by Alvar Aalto.

This Finnish designer had absorbed the principles of Thonet's bentwood furniture (see Chapter Eight, Victorian Vignettes), and the tubular steel furniture of Marcel Breuer (who spread the influence of the Bauhaus in his designs of the 1930s) and Mies van der Rohe (who succeeded Walter Gropius as director of the Bauhaus in 1936 and emigrated to America in 1938). Breuer's most successful design, put into production by the firm of Isokon, was his own clever version of the chaise longue, which exploited the springiness of laminated wood. Aalto experimented with combinations of metal and wood before concentrating on laminated birch as a strong and resilient material, suitable for cantilevered designs and pleasing in appearance. Mr Philp found an apposite reference in *The Architectural Review* following an exhibition of Finnish furniture at Fortnum's in London, in 1933; in his account the magazine's editor wished that the furniture on exhibition would 'spell the death to fake Queen Anne'. Aalto's two best-known chairs, manufactured under the Finmar label, were his armchair, designed around 1930 for the Paimio Sanatorium, and his cantilevered 'Viipuri' armchair of 1933, designed for the Viipuri library but planned for the purposes of mass-production.

'Amid the variety of chairs designed during the era of Modernism, there was little alternative of interest to the most strikingly *avant-garde*, and this was certainly not to everyone's liking', Philippe Garner has written (*Art & Antiques*, March 26, 1978). Such reservations are not unique when dealing with chairs of this period; Mr Philp, for his part, acknowledged the recognition of 'a human need for furniture to be a little less austere than that provided by...Gropius's Bauhaus functionalism, F. Lloyd Wright's "integral" eccentricities or Le Corbusier's "equipment"'. Mr Garner explained: 'The coldness of metal furniture and the bareness of laminated wood were in direct conflict with the accepted notion of well-upholstered comfort. It was not until after the Second World War that a new idea of Modernism appeared, bringing with it new and seductive chair designs.' During the 1950s, he observed, a style emerged which took the uncluttered surfaces of Modernism, its self-conscious functionalism and essential simplicity, but reinterpreted the basic forms, softening the angles and achieving a refined curvilinear style that epitomized all the best features of the design movements of the preceding half century.

Two leaders of 1950s Modernism stand out: one is Eero

Saarinen, son of the Finnish architect Eliel Saarinen; the other is the
American Charles Eames. In 1956 Saarinen designed the 'Tulip'
chair, an organic form in moulded fibreglass and aluminium, which
was mounted on a slender, tapering pedestal support of white-
lacquered cast metal, as fragile-looking as a flower stem. The single-
stem idea was to be seen in Eames's Lounge Chair, in which a
columnar support was the basis for laminated rosewood and buttoned
hide comfort, a chair that was both functional and expressed the dash
and spirit of a new post-war age.

This selective survey of twentieth-century chairs must include
Lloyd Loom furniture, in the doldrums of fashion for several decades,
but now considered 'smart' – with rising prices to match its newfound popularity. When the Museum of the Moving Image (MOMI)
was opened at the South Bank, London, in 1988, to a fanfare of
publicity, a charming corner attracted more than its share of

*ABOVE The simplistic beauty of Art Deco,
seen in a settee of ample proportions and
harmonious lines.*

admiring attention. This was the re-recreation of the appearance, spirit and feel of a picture-house tea-room from the days of the great cinemas in city and surburbia. The author's good friend, Ron Knee, cinemaphile, collector and worshipper at the shrine of twentieth-century nostalgia, was the consultant who provided the artefacts to furnish this niche of memories – or, wherever necessary, commissioned harmonious modern accessories in the old mood. The Lloyd Loom style of furniture was essential to the successful completion of his task, and Mr Knee's questing abilities (allied to a passionate determination to 'get it right') were up to the challenge. He has turned back the reel for those generations of cinema-goers who have often sat in Lloyd Loom chairs in the balcony tea-room, sustaining themselves on Welsh rarebit or Vienna steaks while waiting for the double-feature from Hollywood.

RIGHT A modernist chromium-plated tubular steel armchair designed by Le Corbusier in collaboration with Pierre Jeanneret and Charlotte Perriand.

Lloyd Loom furniture consists of woven 'fibre' chairs, settees and tables. It is named after Marshall B. Lloyd (1858-1927), who manufactured wicker prams at Menominee, Michigan, when furnishings and other objects of wicker and reed were very popular with the late-nineteenth century public. All wicker furniture was handmade, and the process was time- and labour-consuming. Several attempts to weave wicker by machine failed. Then, in 1917, Lloyd invented a machine which could weave 30 times more materials a day than could the fastest skilled handworker. His Lloyd Loom fabric was not wicker, however. The 'fibre' was a paper twisted and woven into cloth, the warp being reinforced by thin steel wire, thus giving the constructions remarkable strength and durability. Students of Lloyd Loom are uncertain whether the steel component was in the original Lloyd invention, or whether it was added later, possibly by W. Lusty and Sons, the exclusive producers of the furniture in England. Lusty's selling line was: 'A heart of steel in every upright strand'.

Chairs were ideal vehicles for the Lloyd Loom technique. They had various kinds of seats. The cheapest were wire-wool or horsehair covered with fabric such as crushed velvet. Next in price were plywood drop-in seats with a thin layer of rubberized foam covered with fabric. The most expensive type was a spring seat with the fabric-covered foam atop. New models were created by changing the shape of the legs or the general look of the under-tier. In addition to seat and table furniture, Lloyd Loom linen baskets proliferated. In 1922 Lusty produced a writing desk 'suitable for the garden room or sun parlour'. In the 1930s there were also hat-stands (*de rigueur* for cinema tearooms) and waste-paper baskets.

The chairs 'with a heart of steel' found employment in many settings, ranging from the lounges of ocean liners to dentists' waiting rooms. One wartime photograph shows RAF fighter pilots relaxing – courtesy of Mr Lloyd or Mr Lusty – at an airfield between alerts during the Battle of Britiain. After the war Lloyd Loom was consigned by the ton to the scrap-heap or it was banished to store sheds. Fortunately, much has survived intact and today it is warmly welcomed in the salerooms and furniture shops; especially desirable are suites of chairs and settees which are in demand for garden-room and conservatory living or designer-penthouse schemes of furnishing.

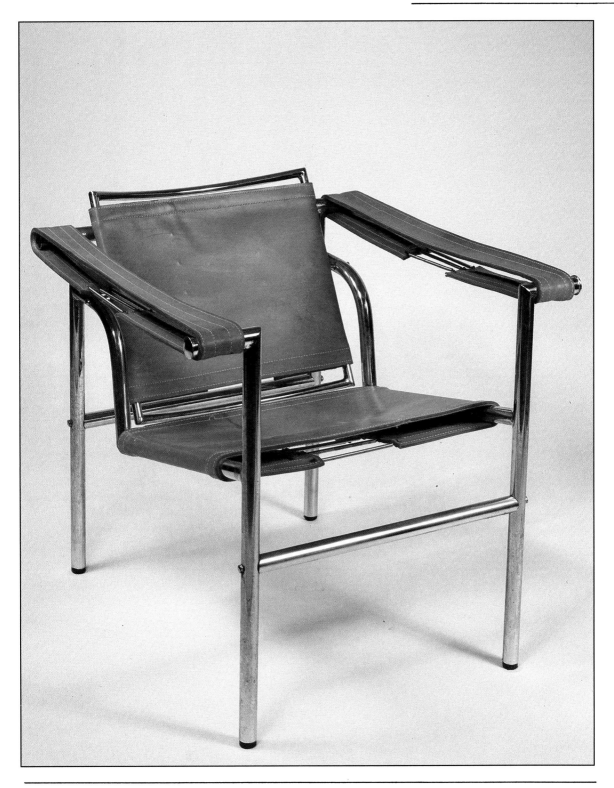

Chapter Fourteen
Seating Baby

Just as chairs for grown-ups developed from benches and stools, so the first seat furniture for children was of the stool variety. In England the earliest high chairs were Elizabethan. They allowed the growing child to take part in the communal life at the family table and eliminated back-bending discomfort for the mother or nurse at feeding times. They were commodious, as was the Elizabethan baby's dress. Seldom was a restraining bar used at the front, as these chairs were meant to be placed against the dinner table, whose solid oak top was in itself sufficient restraint for the child. In any case, it was not the custom to leave babies sitting around; when young children were not sleeping, mothers and nurses tended them in low-seated nursing chairs, with back support and no arms.

Seventeenth-century nursing chairs of oak often had a box seat with a drawer in which to keep nursing requirements. They had panelled backs with a slight rake for the woman's comfort. By the eighteenth century rockers were added. Inevitably miniature versions of these nursing chairs were made specially for children's use, and a further development was the placing of a hole in the chair-seat and the addition of a pewter or earthenware pot where the drawer would be. Rockers on potty chairs were regarded as a natural aid to the child's mental and physical senses of well-being when engaged in this important domestic exercise.

Chair styles were mirrored in miniature for succeeding generations of children. The high chair presented the designer with certain difficulties and challenged his ingenuity. In following the fashion of the cabriole leg, the problem was one of proportion. A high chair standing on stilt-like cabriole legs would be unbalanced in appearance. One solution, as devised by a furniture-maker of around 1745, was to place at each corner of the seat two cabriole legs, one above the other, the result being somewhat weird, but at least acceptable aesthetically.

On the whole, however, children's high-chair design followed more orthodox lines. An oak baby chair of around 1660, in the Victoria & Albert Museum, has knobbed legs united at the bottom by similar stretchers. The uprights are inclined outwards for stability, and the gently tapering effect, as the eye travels upwards, is pleasing. The seat is a sunken panel typical of the time (it would require a cushion), and the back is topped by three turned finials, although many children's chairs had crested backs similar to adults' chairs. There is no restraining rail so the chair was obviously meant to be placed against the table when in use; but there is a foot-rest at conveniently short distance from the baby's seat. This foot-rest was by no means universal in high chairs of that time or even later, and seems to have been included or omitted at the will of the designer. The collector must remember, however, that foot-rests and restraining bars may have disappeared with time and their absence is

by no means a sure guide to age; where they have existed and have been lost, there is usually evidence of attachment.

By the end of Charles II's reign in 1685 high chairs of walnut appeared in a fine, richly carved style imitative of adults' chairs and employing attractive use of cane panels in seats and backs. A typical example would have acanthus-carved cresting on the back and on the deep front stretcher, also incorporating a winged cherub's head in each place.

Influences of the main eighteenth-century designers – Chippendale, Hepplewhite and Sheraton among them – are seen in later children's chairs. The double cabriole leg chair described earlier has a carved splat and back reminiscent of Chippendale, and by this time the upholstered seat was being used. Upholstery, however, was not entirely practical for baby chairs because of wetting. It was far more advisable to employ a wooden seat which could be softened by a loose, washable cushion.

The ladder-back, of horizontal splats, lent itself harmoniously to juvenile needs and the eighteenth century also saw some beautiful examples of the Windsor chair being developed for children, in both high and low varieties. A Windsor high chair of around 1770 is in most respects a microcosm of an adult Windsor but on lengthened legs and with the addition of a foot-rest. The splat bearing the design of a perforated star was common in England at this time and many juvenile chairs were to be found with it. America, which experimented excitingly with the Windsor, produced delightful examples for children. In the Metropolitan Museum, New York, is a superb juvenile Windsor chair of the late-eighteenth century of the comb-back variety: several spindles are extended above the main back in the form of an old-fashioned high comb. There was also the diminutive version of the uniquely American writing-arm Windsor, rare enough in its full-scale example and predictably highly priced in miniature: This chair combined a flat writing arm on the right, underneath which was a small drawer for quills and inks, together with another storage box under the seat. Such a little masterpiece of the late-eighteenth century can command thousands of pounds.

By the dawn of the Victorian age children of the well-to-do were less restricted to the confines of special nursery quarters and were living their young lives increasingly in the company of adults. Therefore their furniture was becoming more sophisticated and miniaturized versions of that being used by their parents were beginning to appear.

Before dealing with Victorian furniture, however, mention should be made of a child's chair which owed its invention to an early-nineteenth century surgeon, Astley Cooper. Imbued with ideas of discipline and correction, Astley Cooper recommended his chair 'with a view of preventing children from acquiring a habit of leaning forward, or stooping; the upright position of the back affording support when the child is placed at table and eating, which a sloping backed chair does not'. It was a tall chair on slightly splayed, turned legs. Its back, as described, was bolt upright and there were no arms to encourage lolling. Perhaps its only concession to juvenile comfort

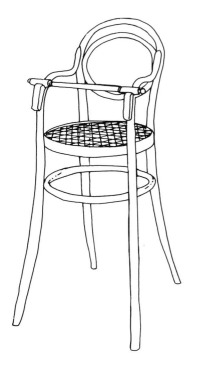

ABOVE *A child's bentwood high chair with caned seat, dating from around 1870.*

were the gently curved horizontal splats. This chair, beloved of bossy governesses and hated by generations of children, became widely accepted for a prolonged period before a more humane outlook finally won through.

Even as late as 1900 a fiendish restraining chair was favoured in town and country. It resembled more a magistrate's court dock than a chair, being simply an open-topped, panelled box of pine or oak, with a plain wooden seat inside. The front was hinged and locked with a clasp on the outside, quite beyond the reach of the imprisoned child.

But such horror stories do a disservice to the Victorians, who produced much charming children's furniture: diminutive suites of wicker armchairs and settees, and delicate nursery items in *papier mâché* and bentwood. The basic high chair, which had taken an important step forward towards the end of the eighteenth century, was developed ingeniously with the invention of the two-part chair; the upper part being an elbow chair with rounded cane back, restraining bar and foot rest; the lower part being a small table. As a high chair the two parts were screwed together; separate, they became table and chair. A nineteenth-century development of this type was the chair with sprung supports between the two halves, thus allowing baby to bounce up and down. A further elaboration was the hinged dining tray which could be detached. Also appearing at this time was the three-function chair: a mechanically minded age was proud of its high chair which, at the depression of a lever, could be reduced to a low chair by outward extension of the legs, and which, by a further adjustment, could be converted into a stable rocker. Examples of this chair are fairly common as they were manufactured until well into this century

The safety of the child was a prime concern when *The Lady's Delight*, a publication of 1715, referred to babies' bones being 'as soft as wax'. More than two and a half centuries later, Benjamin Spock, the world's leading popular authority on child care, advised: 'Falling out of a high chair is a common accident. If you are going to use a high chair, get one with a broad base (so that it doesn't tip over easily) and a strap to buckle the baby in.' Terms of expression apart, designs have not changed much.

ASH

CHERRY

BEECH

CHESTNUT, HORSE

BIRCH

CHESTNUT, SWEET

CEDAR

ELM

LIME

OAK, BROWN

MAHOGANY

OAK, ENGLISH

MAPLE, BIRD'S EYE

PEAR

OAK, AUSTRALIAN

PINE

PLANE

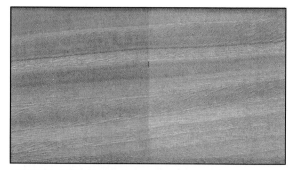

WALNUT, AUSTRALIAN

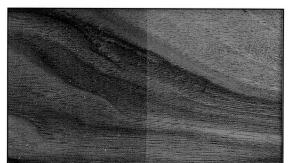

PURPLEWOOD

WALNUT, BLACK AMERICAN

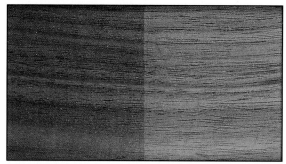

ROSEWOOD, INDIAN

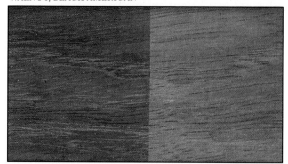

WALNUT, EUROPEAN

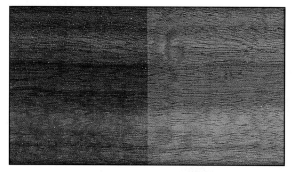

SATINWOOD, EAST INDIAN

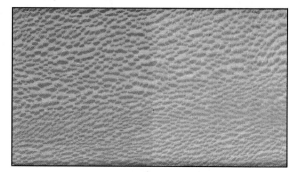

ZEBRAWOOD

Chapter Fifteen
Chair Sense

An affluent Texan tourist, shopping in London, strolled into a saleroom one Monday morning while an auction of furniture and general antiques was in progress. She took a fancy to the chair, ticketed with its lot number, on which she sat, and bought it on impulse when its turn came up. It was a little more expensive than she had hoped, but for all that it was a nice trophy to take home with her on the plane. The extent of her excess baggage became clear when she paid up and discovered, to her shock, that she had also bought seven other chairs: the chair which had caught her fancy was one of a *set* of eight late-Victorian balloon-back diners.

The moral of this anecdote, relished and polished in the trade as a classic stranger-in-the-saleroom story, is: learn the rules. And a cardinal rule, when buying at auction, is to read the catalogue. Not that the experience did Mrs Texas any harm in the long run; her £100 chance investment of the early 1970s, when Victoriana was taking off, left her sitting on a comfortable rosewood nest-egg.

Nevertheless, there are ground rules to learn about investing in antiques and art. 'Never, *never*, buy an antique solely as an investment', was the unwavering advice of Ken Brendling, who was a Phillips saleroom porter in London with 40 years' experience and as much 'inside' knowledge about furniture as any pin-striped specialist in the golden mile of Mayfair. 'Buy something because you like it and it's good. It may do its job as a clock, a carpet, a chair, or simply as decoration. The only dividend your investment will pay is the pleasure or use you get out of it. And, after some time, if you sell at a real profit – which is more than likely – look on that as a bonus.' Mr Brendling's caveat notwithstanding, antique chairs are generally a good investment. Buy a new chair or table or any other piece of furniture from a shop in the High Street and as soon as you get it home its value is reduced to a fraction of what you paid. Buy an antique or old piece of furniture and the value is likely to stay up and, hopefully, go up.

There are some basic tips for buying chairs at auction (some of them can be applied or amended for doing business at the shop of an antique dealer). First, buy the catalogue. Monitor one or two sales to 'feel' the prices before taking the plunge. Get to know chairs by going to saleroom views, where you can handle the goods and closely inspect their construction – something you will not be able to do in a museum. Having read the catalogue, seek the advice of the experts – it's free. Be aware that repairs or elaborate re-upholstery can sometimes cost as much as the original purchase. Measure the piece you are planning to buy: failing to do so can prove a costly mistake if you subsequently disover that it will not fit the place you had in mind for it. If you are bidding personally at auction be sure to set yourself a firm limit, as the speed of a big-city sale can encourage you to bid higher than you may have wished. If you cannot attend the sale personally, or you do not relish the hurly-burly of bidding, you may leave your bid with the auctioneer who will endeavour to secure your lot for you as inexpensively as possible within your limit, taking into account the lot's reserve price and the competition from all the other keen bidders.

In buying chairs, there is a mathematical formula to be learned: large – or as the trade says, 'long' – sets are more valuable *pro rata* than small numbers or singles. 'Long sets of chairs generally cause a stir at auction and the set of 12 which came up at this specialist furniture sale [at Henry Spencer in the east Midlands of England] proved no exception', reported that excellent weekly publication, *Antiques Trade Gazette*, bible to the collector and the professional dealer alike. 'A top estimate of £5,000 had been placed upon the set of 12 early-nineteenth century ebonized open armchairs, with rectangular cane backs, reeded scrolling arms and sabre front supports...The set sold to the Northern trade for £10,000.' An excellently informed resumé of the mathematical price formula of long sets of chairs was to be found in the magazine *Antique Collector* in March, 1980. Graham Shearing wrote: 'What normally happens is that one chair costs £100, two chairs cost £250, three chairs cost £300 (because they do not constitute a set in the usual sense of the word), four chairs will cost £500 – perhaps £600. A set of eight such chairs may cost £1,500 to £2,000. A set of 12 chairs will cost very much more. The reason for this is simply that large sets are so very much rarer, and so the greater rarity value will be reflected in the price.'

What should the collector with modest means do? 'If he needs a large set quickly he will perhaps buy a set of country chairs. If not there are a number of alternatives.' Mr Shearer suggested that the first of these alternatives is to build up a harlequin set, meaning a group of chairs of somewhat differing designs, but with a unifying feature (this could be anything from forms of backs to a common element, such as country rush-seats). 'Secondly he can build up a perfect set from singles and pairs. To do this he will be well advised to choose a well known and common style, for instance a Queen Anne walnut chair with a vase splat and plain cabriole legs of about 1710. By carefully matching he can create a valuable set (although it will be a "matched" set, which in theory is not as good as an original set).' Mr Shearer's third alternative is in effect an extension of the second: to buy a set of four or six, and match it with a pair of elbow chairs, or even another set of four or six. 'But the collector should be advised that it takes time and patience to match a set – dealers know this very well. In most cases the collector will be satisfied with near misses. Experience tells us that few visitors notice small differences.'

Walnut, especially when used as a veneer, does not stand up to the punishment of modern central heating as successfully as the hardy mahogany does; and in this respect oak performs even better than mahogany, undoubtedly a factor in the noticeable rise in popularity of old oak on the North-American market during recent decades. Singing the praises of English oak, a specialist dealer in Kent had this warning to impart: 'Fine oak chairs are always difficult to obtain. One could fill one's shop with pieces that have been messed about with. Try finding an original seventeenth-century masterpiece, and that's a different matter. Oak is still the thing to put your money on, but examples have just got to be *right*. An over-restored piece can be virtually worthless to anyone who knows anything about oak.'

Old oak has a 'bloom' which is almost impossible for the forger to copy. Only experience, however, will enable the collector to recognize this appearance. The look comes from the processes to which the wood was subjected, basically an application of varnish mixed with oil, which sank into the wood and was not merely a surface preservative like that in the nineteenth century. A similar treatment was sometimes given to early-eighteenth century beech to give it an 'oak' look. The modern faker – or honest restorer attempting to match, say, a replaced stretcher with the rest of the chair – will try to simulate the old bloom by discolouring new oak with ammonia, followed up with preparations which include the use of beeswax. One safeguard to alert a potential buyer to this practice is to inspect the under edges of the wood, with their tell-tale 'new' look. Above all, the prospective purchaser should make a friend of a trusted dealer. There are many in the trade, and their reputation and livelihood depend on good customers coming back for more.

The rising value of chairs, as with any other furniture or antique possessions, underlines the importance of having up-to-date insurance valuations. Fire or other disaster can strike anywhere, and the modern burglar keeps up with the prices of antiques through the trade press and an eye on the market. One function of the trade press, sadly, is to keep apace with the burglar, and 'Stolen' notices are a common sight. Surely, chairs and tables are not obvious targets for the burglar, you might ask. Doesn't he prefer silver, jewellery, paintings sliced from the frame? Well, the answer is that, on the whole, he does choose something of a portable nature, but fork-lift theft is thriving, too. Half-ton fonts have disappeared from churches, fireplaces go missing from listed houses under refurbishment, and ponderous garden statuary has to be deeply cemented in or securely bolted down (and even then, the technological-age thief finds a way to spirit it from gardens in the night).

As this chapter is being written, before the author is a clipping from *Antiques Trade Gazette*. It tells of 11 Windsor chairs having been stolen from a house in Buckinghamshire... 'All were painted slate blue although the original eighteenth-century light green colour is underneath', and there is a fairly detailed description of the chairs' form and salient points. Most importantly, the owner had had them photographed, a factor which can help enormously the chances of recovery when the pictures are circulated to police and published for the trade. Owners are strongly advised to photograph their possessions, furniture included; keep detailed descriptions (the original catalogue entry if they were purchased at auction); mark the goods (the local crime prevention police officer can advise methods); and have prudent insurance based on an up-to-date valuation.

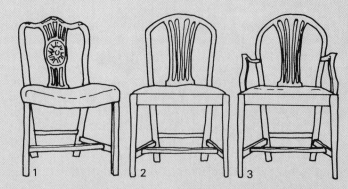

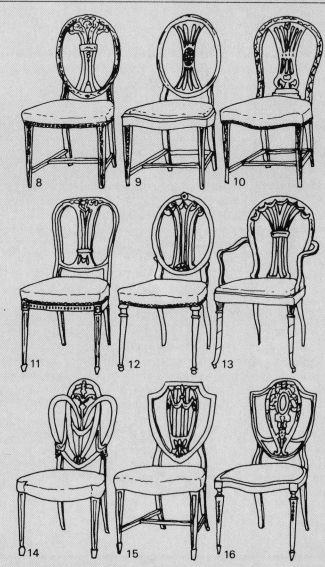

1 Variation of the serpentine top rail with wheel or sun motif in the splats, dipped seat, square legs and stretcher rails.

2,3 Two versions of the hoop back with simple pierced splat and tapered legs.

4 Serpentine top rail with pierced splat, elbow rests and tapered legs.

5,6 Two versions showing the shaped top rail with round shoulders.

7 Shield-shaped back with pierced splat.

8-16 A selection of chair designs illustrating the oval, hoop, interlaced shield or heart and shield backs with various central splats.

17-22 Six designs for chair backs taken from the third edition of The Cabinet-Maker and Upholsterer's Guide, *1794.*

23 An armchair showing the influence of the Louis XV style.

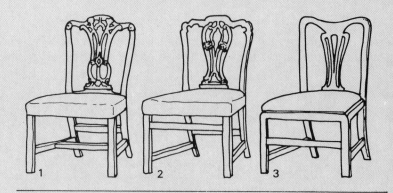

1-7 *Chippendale chair designs illustrating various pierced central splats, the interlaced and the ladderback. There are several different arrangements of the stretcher rails but they were usually fitted as shown in 6 and 7.*

8 *The cover of Chippendale's* One Hundred and Thirty-three Designs, *London 1834.*

9, 10 *Two examples of chairs in the Chinese or lattice style.*

11/12 *Two examples of Chippendale's more ornate work with sweeping lines and intricate ribband designs.*

8

1-10 Sheraton chairs of the early-nineteenth century showing various treatments of the rectangular backs.

11-22 Chair backs published by Sheraton in his Drawing Book, illustrating the predominance of the rectangular style and the adaptation of the lyre form and the shield shape.

23 Design for a drawing room chair, published by T. Sheraton, April 1804, showing signs of the French Empire influence.

24, 25 Armchairs — Sheraton usually used marquetry for decoration, but he used inlaid brass as an ornament in his later work. Generally the decoration was in wreaths of flowers, husks or drapery.

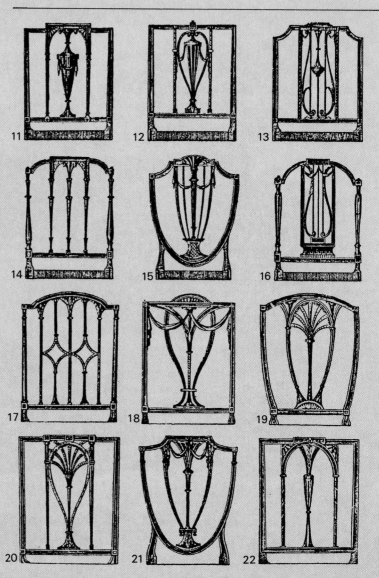

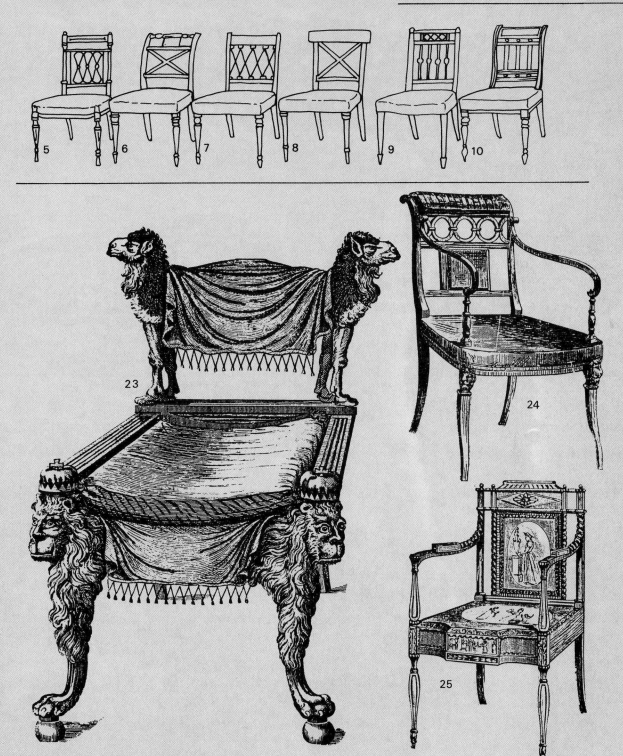

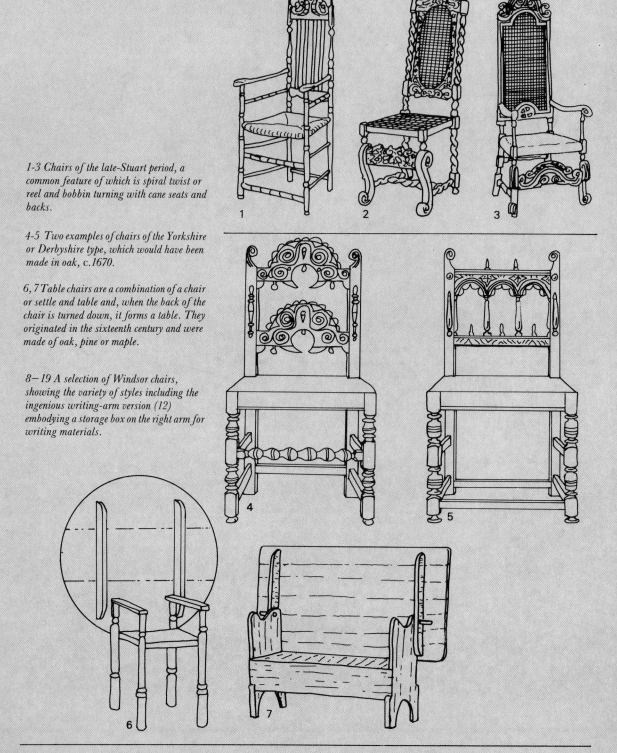

1-3 Chairs of the late-Stuart period, a common feature of which is spiral twist or reel and bobbin turning with cane seats and backs.

4-5 Two examples of chairs of the Yorkshire or Derbyshire type, which would have been made in oak, c.1670.

6, 7 Table chairs are a combination of a chair or settle and table and, when the back of the chair is turned down, it forms a table. They originated in the sixteenth century and were made of oak, pine or maple.

8—19 A selection of Windsor chairs, showing the variety of styles including the ingenious writing-arm version (12) embodying a storage box on the right arm for writing materials.

1 A sixteenth-century oak box stool.

2 A long stool of carved walnut of the Louis XV period.

3 A seventeenth-century oak joint stool.

4 Details of turning of stool legs in use throughout the first half of the seventeenth century.

5,6,7 Three examples showing the typical style of Morris & Co chair production of the late-nineteenth/early-twentieth centuries — honest country style and rush-seated elegance, classics of fine craftsmanship.

8-11 A selection of ladder or slat-back chairs. Mainly country styles from America and dating from the late-eighteenth and nineteenth centuries.

12, 13 Nineteenth-century Boston rockers, customarily bearing painted and stencilled decoration.

14 A variety of Shaker chair finials showing some of their common features.

15 Shaker rocking chair illustrating the scrolled arms and short, blunt 'sled' rockers of the early period.

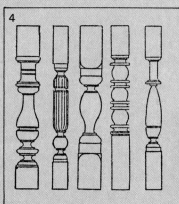

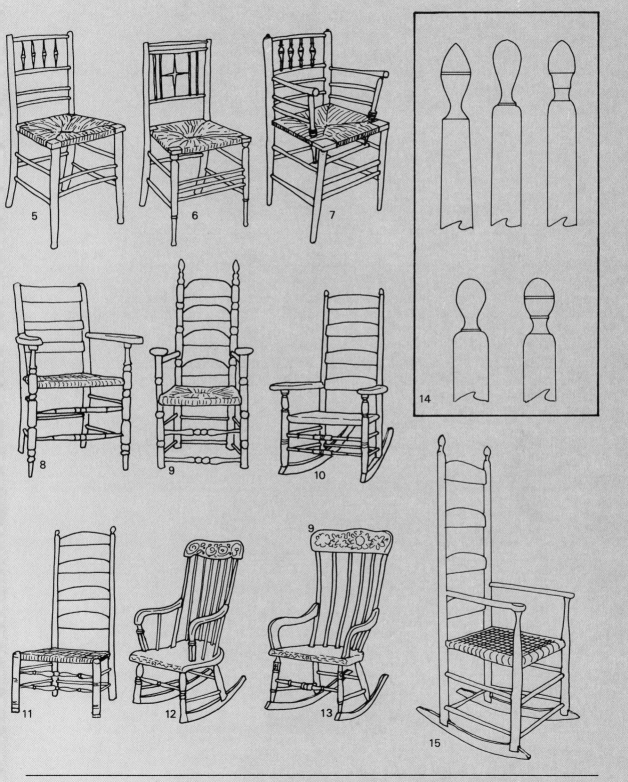

1 Armchair with covered seat and back from the early-seventeenth century. The front legs and arm supports are turned.

2 Early-Georgian wing chair with carved cabriole legs and ball-and-claw feet.

3 A chair of X-frame construction, covered in fabric and studded with ornamental nailing.

4 Armchair by Chippendale with pierced stretcher rails.

5 Carved mahogany armchair by Chippendale, c.1760.

6 A cock-fighting chair — the gentleman would straddle the seat, resting his elbows on the arms and facing the back of the chair. Similar versions were made for reading and were fitted with a book-rest, candle bracket and a drawer in each arm, to store pipes and tobacco.

7 Early-Victorian chair with button back known as a 'nursing' or 'ladies' chair.

8 Early-Victorian armchair with button back often called a 'grandmother chair'.

9 Mahogany armchair by Chippendale in the Chinese style, c.1755.

10 The curving grace of a Thonet bentwood rocking chair is shown in this example of the late-nineteenth century.

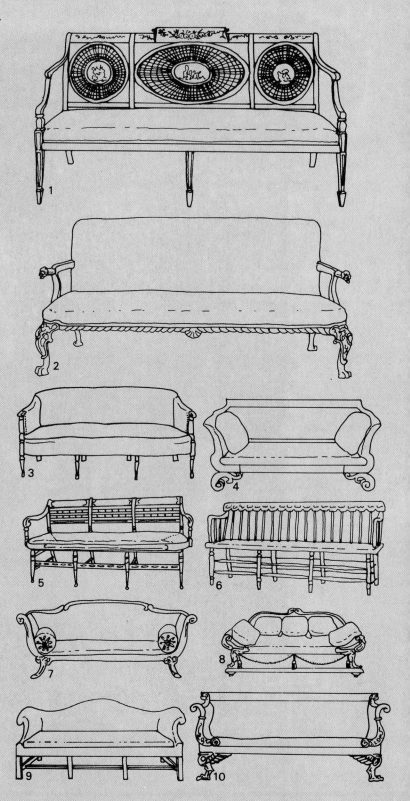

1 Late-Sheraton settee with square tapered legs and spade feet. The medallions in the back panels and the rail are decorated with painted subjects.

2 Chippendale settee with the arms terminating in carved lions' heads. The cabriole legs have cabochons on the knees and lion-paw feet.

3-10 Some of the wide variety of sofa designs available during the nineteenth century. American styles tended to trail European notions, but sofas and settees of outrageous form were particularly popular in America.

11 Design for a sofa, titled Confidante, taken from Hepplewhite's Guide.

12 Design for a couch, titled Duchesse, taken from Hepplewhite's Guide.

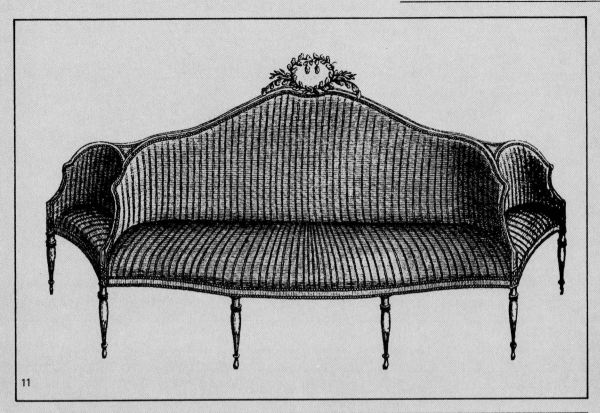

11

12

Glossary

Acanthus
The leaf of the acanthus tree became a design motif in ancient Greek art and was later revived in Renaissance design. Chippendale, among many eighteenth-century furniture designers, included carved acanthus leaves on the knees of cabriole-leg chairs.
(illus)

Ball foot
Turned foot, somewhat spherical; used in the late-seventeenth century.

Balloon-back chair
A type extremely popular in Victorian times, incorporating an oval or round back of continuous line.

Baluster
A short pillar with a curving outline resembling a vase shape.

Banding
A band of contrasting colour or material used decoratively, especially in veneer and marquetry.

Banister-back chair
A tall-backed chair with curving outline resembling a vase shape.

Baroque
Originating in Italy, this was a style derived from the classical, but altogether more dynamic. The restraint of classical form was abandoned in favour of the sumptuous features, characterized by sweeping lines and swirling scrolls. In retaining the basic precepts of Renaissance design — columns, pediments and a certain symmetry — while losing the pure classical proportions, the baroque was a heavy and ornate architectural style. Baroque furniture designs are also marked by heavily ornamented features.

Bead or beading
Narrow, semi-circular moulding.

Bergère
In France the term usually refers to low-backed armchairs with upholstered sides and cushions. In England, a *bergère* is a chair with caned panels in its back, arms and seat.

Berlin woolwork
A popular Victorian wool needlework depicting flowers, landscapes and pastoral scenes, sometimes used in small screens.

Bun foot
Resembles a flattened globe, used in the late-seventeenth century.

Cabriole (bandy) leg
Popular in the late-seventeenth century and throughout the eighteenth century, a cabriole leg curves outwards at the knee and inwards again at the foot. Its elongated S-form is gently tapered towards the base. The word is derived from the Latin, *caper* — goat.

Cartouche
An ornately framed panel often set in the back of a chair and decorated with armorial devices or a painted scene.

Chamfer
A bevelled edge: an edge that has been cut away from the square or smoothed down.

Chesterfield
An over-stuffed settee, of the type popular in the 1920s.

Chinoiserie
A pseudo-Chinese style developed in Europe and popular throughout the eighteenth century. The vogue for Chinese motifs — pagodas, lattice work and fretwork — represented one aspect of the ornamental rococo style.

Claw-and-ball foot
Probably originated in China and said to have represented the three-clawed foot of a dragon clutching a pearl; introduced into England from Holland in the late-seventeenth century and much used in conjunction with the cabriole leg in the eighteenth century.

Club foot
The simplest terminal to a cabriole leg used on chairs in the eighteenth century.

Comb-back chair
An early version of the hoop-back Windsor chair, dating from the mid-eighteenth century. It was formed of spindles rising from the seat and passing through the horseshoe-shaped rail at the back.

Cowhorn or crinoline stretcher
Characteristic of some Windsor chairs, this was a semi-circular rail connecting the two front legs and itself connected by two short rails to the back legs.

Dipped seat
A concave-shaped seat — the sides being higher than the saddle.

Ears
A small bracket-like scroll shape added to the top of a cabriole leg to continue the curve of the knees.

Empire style
The neo-classical style of architecture and design created practically by edict of Napoleon; based on the imperial forms of ancient Greece, Rome and Egypt. It influenced furniture designers throughout Europe and in America for three to four decades in the first half of the nineteenth century.

Federal style
An American term that describes furniture from the United States made in the 1785-1830 period, during the early days of the Republic. Federal styles are reminiscent of Sheraton and Hepplewhite designs.

Fiddle back or splat
A splat resembling the outline of a fiddle found in walnut chairs of the early-eighteenth century.

Gesso
A plaster-type substance applied to furniture to provide decorative details in place of carving, and popular in the eighteenth century.

Hoop-back chair
A chair whose uprights and top-rail form a continuous curve.

Hoof-foot
Hoof-shaped base of a leg, representing principally the goat hoof on a cabriole leg.

Inlay
A surface ornament used to decorate furniture. Separate pieces of different woods, bone, ivory, shell, etc., are set into the piece of furniture, in a recessed ground.

Japanning
English term for the decorative process used in imitation of Oriental lacquer; introduced in the late-seventeenth century.

Knee
The uppermost curve of the cabriole leg, where it is thickest.

Lacquer
Decorative process originating in the Orient and based on the use of natural varnish.

Ladder-back chair
A chair with horizontal slats or rails resembling a ladder.

Latticework
Construction in wood or metal of criss-cross design.

Linenfold carving
A carved ornament reminiscent of folded linen. It was particularly popular in Flemish wood carving and remained popular in Tudor and Elizabethan times.

Louis style
This term is used generally to describe French furniture or pieces following a French style. However, it is vague as it can refer to any of three Louis — Louis XIV, Louis XV or Louis XVI — who have all given their names to styles of furniture. The latter two had the greatest influence; the Louis XV style was characteristically rococo, with curving lines and light ornamentation, while the Louis XVI style reacted against this, favouring strong vertical and horizontal lines, a heavier style that revived aspects of classical design.

Lyre-back chair
Name given to chairs in which the design of the back consists of an adaptation of the classical lyre; seen in designs of Adam and Sheraton.

Marquetry
An inlaid veneer of different woods used to decorate furniture. It became popular in Europe from the seventeenth century onwards. Dutch marquetry was particularly fine.

Ormolu
Gilded bronze, much used during the seventeenth and eighteenth centuries by the French for decorative mounts to furniture.

Overstuffed seat
A chair seat in which the upholstery is carried over the seat rail and secured beneath it.

Pad foot
A simple terminal to a cabriole leg resembling the club foot in shape but resting on a small pad or disc.

Paw foot
A base of a leg representing an animal's paw, usually a lion's. An Egyptian motif found in fashionable English furniture of the first half of the eighteenth century; used to limited extent in some Regency designs.

Palladian style
A style of architecture following the principles adopted by the Italian architect Andrea Palladio (1508-1580). In England during the first half of the eighteenth century the Palladian style was revived. Its popularity signified a rejection of the decadent baroque and return to pure, restrained classicism. Palladian furniture made use of architectural features — cornices and swags.

Patina
The surface or finish resulting on wood from wear, polishing and oxidation with age.

Rail
Horizontal structural member; for example the seat rail of a chair.

Ribbon-back chair
Descriptive term derived from some of Chippendale's chairs in which the openwork back is carved with an elaborate arrangement suggesting entwined ribbons of silk, with bows; mid-eighteenth century.

Rococo
A style of ornamentation developed in France from the Chinese forms in the early-eighteenth century and generally associated with the Louis XV style. Shell, rock and other natural forms dominate the ornament. It followed the Baroque style and was most used by the French and by Chippendale in his adaptation of the French style. The word is derived from two French words — *rocaille* (rock) and *coquille* (shell).

Sabre leg
A sharply carved chair leg; a classical style popular in the late-eighteenth and early-nineteenth centuries.

Scroll foot
Curved like a scroll, often used in association with the cabriole leg, and fashionable in the mid-eighteenth century.

Serpentine shape
An undulating curve adapted to the front of furniture.

Settle
A long wooden seat with an arm at each end and a high panelled back; the lower box-like part was sometimes fitted with drawers or a hinged lid.

Shaker chairs
Made in America by the Shakers, a religious sect, these simple provincial chairs are well-proportioned and substantially made with little or no decoration. They were usually made of pine, maple, walnut or fruit woods.

Shield-back
Descriptive term for a chair-back design, much favoured by Hepplewhite in the 1780s, and his disciples even to Edwardian days.

Slat
Thin horizontal bar of a chair back. In chairs of the Queen Anne period the slats were often solid.

Spade foot
A short tapered foot, used on the square tapered supports to furniture of the late-nineteenth century.

Spiral turning
Descriptive term for legs or stretchers of the Restoration period in which the typical 'barley-sugar' twist was much used.

Splat
The central vertical part of an open chair back.

Squab
Loose cushion, much used before upholstered furniture became general.

Stick-back
Informal name for the traditional Windsor chair.

Strapwork
A carved ornamental geometric design with narrow bands crossed and interlaced. It was particularly popular in late-Elizabethan and Jacobean decoration.

Stretcher
A rail connecting and bracing the legs of a chair or table. With cabriole-leg chairs stretchers disappeared, to be revived in the Hepplewhite period.

Stringing
Extremely narrow line or lines of veneer; used to good effect as light and dark stringing on eighteenth-century satinwood furniture.

Veneer
A veneer is a thin layer of wood applied to a piece of furniture. This is a process aimed at achieving decorative effects that would be impossible if solid panels of wood were used. Veneering was introduced in the late-seventeenth century when walnut became popular; it was widely used throughout the following two centuries. Originally, wood was cut to 3 mm (⅛inch) thickness by hand-saw. Much later machines were used to cut the wood even finer. The veneer showed up the grain of the wood; pieces were carefully matched, then polished to give a rich hue.

Wing-chair
Easy chair, usually upholstered, with ear-pieces or 'wings' to the back; popular at most periods from the late-seventeenth century onwards.

Index

Page numbers in italic refer to illustrations.